For you Mom,

love

5/12/13

Joy, Interrupted

An Anthology on Motherhood and Loss

Edited by Melissa Miles McCarter

Contributors:

Merrill Edlund - Aliki Economides - Monika Pant
Grace Benedict - Chris Reid - Paul Salvette
Terri Elders - Liz Dolan - Mark Moore - Ivan Jim Saguibal Layugan
Lottie Corley - Sandra Kolankiewicz - Megan Moore
Valerie Murrenus Pilmaier - Anna Steen - Nina Bennett
Kim Hensley Owens - Joanne L. DeTore - Ione Citrin - Emily Polk
Robyn Parnell - Danelle - Svetlana Bochman - Erin Williams
Gail Marlene Schwartz - Olivia Good - Elynne Chaplik-Aleskow
Margaret Kramar - Carol Alexander - Valean Iolanda
Melissa Miles McCarter - Samantha - Kristin Anderson - Lisa Wendell
Janeen McGuire - Anindita Chatterjee - Jenn Williamson - Mazel Flores
Rebecca Manning - Pooja Sachdeva - Nancy Arroyo Ruffin
Gabriella Burman - Sheila Hageman - Ruth Krongold
G. Karen Lockett Warinsky - Jennifer Molidor - Alan Nolan
Trangđài Glassey-Trầnguyễn - Jemila Modesti - Deborah Finkelstein
Jessica Karbowiak - Ann Mathew - Yolanda Arroyo Pizarro
Mary O'Neill - Lori Lamothe - Michèle AimPée Parent

Fat Daddy's Farm Press
(fatdaddysfarm.org)

ISBN 9780985235604
Library of Congress Control Number: 2012934140

First Paperback Edition

Cover Design by Fat Daddy's Farm
Front: "Adieu Maman" by Jemila Modesti – Oil
Back: "Broken Chain" by Grace Benedict – Mixed media

This anthology was made possible because of the financial support of Christy Filipich, Glee and David Suntrip, Nayana Jennings, Zoey Mdalel, Sarah Goss, Diana Graham, Terri Ellen Pease, Marisa Elena James, Jocelyn Paige Kelly, Pat Miles, William Matthew McCarter, Lon Miles, Tim Moore, and Erlyne Magnum. Ann Mathew and Ann Mayhew provided editing and proofreading assistance.

There were many people who provided emotional support and guidance throughout the process of editing this book. Special thanks to Sarah Goss, Vicki Sapp, Kevin Gustafson, Melinda Miles Guillory, Linda Guillory, and Lon and Pat Miles.

I would not have been able to edit this anthology without my husband, William Matthew McCarter, who let me be his literary trophy wife and best friend, and my step-son, Britin, who gave me a much needed (and unexpected) chance to mother.

Contents

Longing

Acceptance

Epilogue

Contributors

Dedications

Introduction

Joy comes, grief goes,
we know not how.

James Russell Lowell

"What if "-Michele AimPée Parent

Joy, Interrupted

Joy and grief, that space between's not so far apart. It's actually intertwined. And I know that can be scary. I get that. But it can also give you freedom. There's freedom in knowing you can carry joy and grief together.

- Nancy Berns, TED Talk, 2012

Like so many people who have dealt with loss in their lives, I have been caught in the space between joy and grief since my daughter died of SIDS in 2003, and during my last ten years struggling with secondary infertility. In the course of editing this book I have learned that this space of grief and joy isn't limited to loss, but is part of the act of mothering. Despite barriers to biological motherhood, I will always be in this space of grief and joy because of my role as a step-mother.

The conception of this anthology was inspired by my own grief journey. After the death of my daughter, I was so mired in my pain and disoriented by trauma that making sense out of my experiences was difficult. I found that grief can be myopic and lonely. Sometimes I couldn't see beyond my pain and my pain was not always understood or shared by others.

In trying to cope with the interruption of my joy of motherhood that occurred so dramatically after my daughter's death, I sought solace in writing and reading. Since deciding to be a writer when I was eleven years old, writing had always helped me to make sense out of my world. Writing has helped me to locate myself when the ambiguities of life seemed overwhelming.

I sought solace in the works of others, trying to find other people whose joys of motherhood had been interrupted. (I say interrupted because even with the death of a child we do not lose our identities as mothers, our memories linking us to our children eternally.) In trying to cope with this interruption, I read posts by women in online discussions who had also lost their children to SIDS. There were memoirs about motherhood and loss that were a comfort to me, such as Gloria Vanderbilt's book, "A Mother's Love," about her coping with her young adult son's suicide.

At times, I wanted to relate to women who had similar experiences as mine: women who were grieving the death of their infant, and then, later, women who when struggling infertility. Although not all spoke specifically to my own experiences, I was able to see how pain is pain, no matter the depth or the cause.

I found that there were memoirs, novels, short stories, movies, anthologies, and more that told the tales of mothers whose joys had been interrupted, deferred or delayed. Women who had miscarriages; daughters who talked about the pains of being adopted; women struggling with the loss of identity while mothering; men and women who were taking care of their dying mothers; and more. Seeing the varied dimensions of motherhood and loss was healing for me, helping me feel like I wasn't alone.

Perhaps quixotically and naively, I decided to edit an anthology that dealt with the multiple dimensions of motherhood and loss. I thought it would be easily done in a year, and at first it seemed that way. Pieces from all over the world came pouring in about experiences similar and different from my own. The compiling of pieces wasn't difficult, but the actually editing process was challenging.

Each piece was so poignant, moving and intense that reading them over and over while editing them was often gut-wrenching. In approaching the contributions collectively, I found the process cathartic, but it also took a lot of psychic energy for me to face my grief and those of others repeatedly.

4

Even though it was draining, I found going over and over the contributions aided in my own healing process. I was ripping the bandage off of a wound that had been poisoned by grief, blood-letting to survive.

Editing the anthology also proved to be a paradigm shift. In collecting the contributions for this anthology, including artwork, poetry, prose, creative non-fiction, and flash fiction, I learned to see my experiences in a larger, more universal, context. Some of these universal themes include: coping with the death of a child; relationships between mother and child (including adoption and estrangement): caring for disabled children: and having to mother one's own mother because of an illness. I only had personal experience with a few of these situations; reading about these varied experiences, real and imagined, expanded my consciousness about what it is to mother.

In reading about other dimensions of loss, I saw new opportunities for coping, for making meaning out of pain, and for healing. I watched as the contributors processed (or didn't process) their grief and it helped me see that my own space between grief and joy was wider than I had imagined, with me moving closer and closer to the other side of joy. The contributors to this anthology helped me, as Shakespeare wrote, "give sorrow words." They sometimes said what I wanted to say, but didn't know how. And when they said things I didn't feel, my capacity for compassion grew. I felt connected to these contributors. My pain wasn't boxing me in the space of grief because I felt less alone.

It is my hope that this anthology can do some of the same for readers, allowing for movement closer to the side of joy. I hope this anthology can reveal how each loss reaffirms the many possibilities of motherhood, even when joy is interrupted.

While editing this anthology about motherhood and loss, I have realized that, in every action of mothering, of being mothered, of wanting to mother, we live in the space between joy and grief, sometimes gravitating to one more than the other.

This anthology reflects this space between joy and grief.

Melissa Miles McCarter
May, 2013

Note on Organization & Content:

I divided this anthology in five sections loosely based on the "five stages of grief." The pieces in each section reflect what I felt when reading them. The first section, "No," encompasses the denial and shock we tend to feel in the immediate wake of loss; the second, "Furies" reflects the intensity of anger that can come with loss; the third, "Longing," shows the emptiness and despair we often what we feel in the face of loss; the fourth, "Plea," expresses the wish that loss hadn't occurred; and the last section, "Acceptance," is what happens when we have some peace or resolution after loss.

In terms of content, it was important to me to represent the widest possibilities of motherhood and loss. I wanted international perspectives, whether expressed in "broken" or fluent English. I wanted both the most literary of expositions on the subject and the sentimental rawness of people who would not call themselves writers. I wasn't put off by the inelegant and un-eloquent. At times the pieces didn't reflect where I was or my own perspectives on grief, but this difference was okay and, I think, adds to the breadth of the anthology. I like that the styles vary so much—dark, straightforward, cloaked, ambiguous, sweet; I felt the more variety, the more people the book could speak to. I wanted to show myriad types of loss through the widest array of voices.

Some of my choices might seem unexpected or surprising. I predict readers will think some of my selections should not have been included—or don't understand why I included certain ones. Even when the organization or selection of the pieces seemed to have no rhyme or reason, I trusted my instincts.

One aspect that might seem confusing is why I put certain pieces in certain sections of book. I confess that I didn't always go by what seemed to be the author's intention. For example, an author might have thought her (or his) piece was about acceptance, while I might have felt it to be the opposite, a big fat no. Readers might categorize them differently, having a different conception of a grief journey altogether. But, I do think my selections and organizations have the potential to open up our views about the space between joy and grief, and what the act of mothering can entail. I see this anthology as a prism reflecting a multiplicity of voices. Each voice meant something to me, and I anticipate that some of the pieces will mean something for others, as well.

How to read this book:

In my opinion, anthologies aren't meant to be read straight through. In fact, I welcome readers to dip into this book, rather than reading it cover to cover (although I did do this more than once and believe it is possible for readers to read it straight through.) I have tried to stay true to the grieving experience, or at least my grieving experience, in organizing this book. Many of the pieces in the book are incredibly intense, especially for those who have not suffered the same types of emotional loss as some of the contributors in the book have. And even if you have had similar types of intense loss, there will be people uncomfortable with some of the emotions that these pieces, especially as a whole, can elicit.

You might ask: Where do I start "dipping?" One person suggested I add to the table of contents a short synopsis for each piece and highlight the type of loss the piece features. I don't even know if I could categorize each piece in that way—so much of the experience of loss can't be categorized and what I see won't be what others see when they read each piece.

Instead, I encourage you to select pieces from the table of contents whose titles speak to you. Or, you could randomly pick a place in the book and start reading. I actually favor the second approach because it mirrors so much of the randomness that surrounds a traumatic event. I believe that this random perusal of the book, if you so choose, could open you up to insights that you might not have had if you looked for a piece that fit a certain category. I believe being open to serendipity is an important aspect of healing.

Finally, I hope you will take special care in reading this book, whether dipping or submerging yourself. Editing this book was extremely difficult, emotionally and intellectually (not to mention that managing so many contributors is like herding cats!) It has been a huge risk for me to take on this project, and I hope you believe it was worth taking this chance.

So, please go ahead, dear reader, and take a chance with me....

No

Denial -- is the only fact
Perceived by the Denied --
Whose Will -- a numb significance –
The Day the Heaven died –

Emily Dickinson, "Denial-- is the only Fact"

"Passion Flower" - Grace Benedict
Ink wash & colored pencil

Joy, Interrupted

I always think of denial as covering something up, like the proverbial ostrich hiding his head in the sand. But, this doesn't seem to accurately describe the experience we feel when first faced with a traumatic loss that interrupts our narrative about life. I could never wrap my head around the idea that denial means we just don't believe that a trauma has occurred. I saw denial as a type of resistance--a big fat "no" to reality. No -- that isn't the way life is supposed to be. No -- that hurts too much. No --I can't deal with this. I guess another way to put denial is, "Stop." After a loss, our lives do stop in a sense, and we can't move on from the space of no, sometimes for quite awhile when other people have started again to say yes.

So much of motherhood is saying yes. Yes to life, yes to new possibilities, yes to the future. Our "yes" is interrupted by loss, and this can be doubly hard in light of an experience which, by its nature, is affirmative. This "No" section is modeled after the "first stage of grief" so many of us feel immediately after loss, and get stuck in, or keep coming back to.

There are many different ways to say no and to say yes to loss, and I tried to select a variety of pieces to show these many possibilities.

I started the "No" section with Mary O'Neill's "Foundling" and closed with Danelle's "Still-Life: Embracing the 2009 Voice" because they connected so deeply to my own experience of "no." They are two intense pieces about the death of a child which show very different ways to say no to unexpected loss.

Not all losses are as obvious as death and can just be part of life's transitions we may resist, such as in Anna Steen's "Star Bunk" and Margaret Kramar's "The Dining Hall." They showed me how loss can occur in the act of parenting, even if that loss is "normal." I also saw how each yes can be a transition cloaked in loss, as in Valean Iolanda's "The Cardboard Robots" and G. Karen Lockett Warinsky's "Departure for College."

While selecting the pieces for this section, I kept feeling "no." I felt "no," when I read Anindita Chatterje's "Anirvan: The Deathless One." This might seem confusing -- how could I say no while selecting pieces for the anthology? Wouldn't saying no mean I shouldn't put them in? But I wasn't saying no to the quality of the work; I was saying no to the feelings the works elicited.

There were many feelings and thoughts these pieces elicited, some more comfortable for me than others. Some reflected my own experiences in grieving or the ways I have continued to cope. Sheila Hageman's "Celebrity News" and "Cluttered" reminded me of all the many ways my own life had stopped despite the movements I seemingly made each day. Carol Alexander's "Dandelion Child" elicited in me the visceral aspect of grieving that we may compartmentalize in order to function.

Other pieces explored visions of loss I had not yet experienced, such as when Chris Reid's "Concern Respiration" and Ruth Krongold's "Voices (February 2009)" reveal intense grieving caused by the possibility of loss. These pieces made me face the full force of the grief of others which, normally, I would be uncomfortable thinking about.

In each no, there became the possibility of yes. I saw this possibility, different forms and perspectives of yes, in the Lottie Corley's poem, "Trinkets," and Ann Mathew's analytical essay, "Smoothening the Crumples: Poetry Dancing on Paper through 'Kumina'." They introduced me to two very different ways to frame loss.

This might be the hardest section to read because the stage of no can be when sorrow is most intense. Certainly the sorrow is palpable in many of the pieces, such as in Liz Dolan's "Struck by Lightning." The intensity varies from piece to piece, and I have purposefully interspersed different intensities of grieving because I recognize leaping from sorrow to sorrow can be draining.

I have heard from those in the midst of grieving soon after loss that they didn't want to read anything sorrowful. They are so in the "no" that they can't fully face how the loss has interrupted their narrative. They want everything to be normal, to go back to the way things were before their loss. Rebecca Manning's "The Sign" reminded me of this desire to avoid having our day to day existence interrupted by the grief of others.

Even if you aren't sure if you want to dive into the deep end of sorrow, I think if you give this section a chance, even if it is only to come back to it after exploring the other ones, you might find yourself moving into the space of yes. It might not be the space of yes we associate with acceptance, but the space of possibility. This space might not be the same one you were in before your loss, before joy was interrupted, but maybe it can be a space where lightness can truly exist again, even if it is a different shade and hue.

The writers might or might not associate their pieces with the "no" I was feeling. You the reader might not feel or think "no." But, in my own saying no, I ultimately found myself moving through the sludge of resistance, feeling lighter despite the sorrow that felt like wearing shoes made of bricks.

I believe we muddle through the darkness, through the shadows of no, before we can find that space of yes.

Joy, Interrupted

Foundling
by Mary O'Neill

Lying on the couch I noticed that the cartographic extravaganza that had appeared on the ceiling has expanded from Australia to now include a suggestion of Indonesia. Last night I had pointed out that Australia hadn't been there just a few days beforehand and was definitely a cause for concern. My husband, who is a "not doing" sort, and has very sophisticated strategies for ensuring that his not doing lifestyle is uninterrupted, began to argue that I was geographically deluded and to discuss which country was emerging above our heads as a means of avoiding the obvious – someone needed to check our pipes for leaks. Initially, I allowed myself to be sucked into the map argument, but now there was no option. He was going to have to root about with the pipes upstairs to see where the leak was coming from.

"Pete. It's getting bigger." He wasn't in the room, but we had developed a relationship over the years that involved shouting at each other from different parts of the house. "Pete, there is water pouring through the living room ceiling."

Ah, finally a response. I'm impressed that even after all these years he still believes me, which is a little charming, and a bit worrying. I assumed years ago he would learn that I was a liar, but it always worked. Arriving with the washing-up bowl in his hand that wouldn't have been all that useful had there actually been water coming through the ceiling, he showed a certain willingness to be helpful, which I appreciated.

I am pondering what a pair of fools we are. He falls for my motivating lies and I still think something has happened when he curses loudly. He isn't really a foul-mouthed sort, but when given any kind of tool, he "buggers" and "bollocks" as if he was perpetually injuring himself. Early on, I used to run to wherever he was working to see if I was needed to retrieve a severed finger or apply pressure to a punctured artery. But, he would look at me in surprise, unaware than he had said anything, let alone exclaimed loudly, suggesting serious injury. Now he is uncustomarily and disconcertingly quiet.

Our bedroom has been transformed from a normal comfortable chaos to a complete and very uncomfortable mess. The bed has been pulled towards the door so I have to climb onto it to get into the room. Pete is sitting on the floor at the far side of the bed. He is completely motionless, no swearing, oh God, he must be hurt.

"Pete, what's wrong?" It seems to take forever to climb over all the rubbish from the floor piled onto the bed. A couple of floorboards have been taken up and he is staring into the hole. "Pete." Still not a sound. He has a box in his hands. "Pete, what is it?" I am starting to sound a little shrill because this is so unlike him.

I follow his stare into the box. "Shit, Pete. Oh my god, what is it, Pete." In the box is a creature, or at least the remains of a creature. I can hear myself saying things, but I'm not sure what's coming out. Whatever it is I want it to be gone, for Pete to get rid of it, to talk to me.

"It's a baby," he says. This doesn't help and I feel more hysterical – I need to get out of the room but the bed is between me and the door. Pete reaches out his hand and grabs my leg and tugs. I plop onto the floor beside him. As the hysteria passes the awfulness of what is in the box becomes more real.

We sit there for an eternity. What the hell is happening? Pete gestures the box towards me. It is a shoebox, I guess, so the baby must have been very small. It is wrapped in a cloth that has become threadbare, so I can clearly see the shape of the little body beneath. It is still curled-up as it would have been in the womb, legs tucked up and crossed at the ankles and its hand is to its mouth as if sucking its thumb.

The exposed head and hand look papery, the body must somehow have dried out. The size of the baby suggests it had not reached full term. Unfortunately I know too much about small premature babies, babies that die before ever having reached the air. I have had three of these little creatures, my little fish. The only knowledge I have of them is from my inside, the fluttering and nudging of an aquatic creature growing quietly on its own. Each time I was hopeful, feeling that this one was stronger, showed more will to live. I convinced myself by omens that each confirmed pregnancy had all the elements for success. But each ended at the same stage.

The first feeling of oddness that I would try to dismiss as the thrill of pregnancy, until the spots of pink on my knickers would cruelly look so innocent. It became harder and harder to convince myself that all women have the odd spot of blood. And then, the pain would start and then the bleeding; the real thing, pints of blood running everywhere. I put a towel between my legs and called the ambulance. "No, I can't walk to the front door, no my husband isn't with me, yes, yes, I have phoned him, yes, I am alone."

Completely alone, no more fluttering fish, no more inside pal that has been everywhere with me for weeks, no more chats to my stomach at night. Then there's the stupid little chair that is used to lift you out of the house and into the ambulance. The medics cover me with a blanket, not bothering to look under the towel; there is no point, it is obvious. The young smooth faced doctors in the A and E who don't really want to get involved because they haven't done their obstetrics and gynecology yet, put me in a side room on a narrow and uncomfortable bed. Eventually a registrar comes in and asks if I have passed anything yet. It takes a while to realise he is talking about my baby. The first time I innocently say I don't know. The second and third time I know that if you don't know, you haven't. Because when your baby comes out you know it.

It may not be as physically painful as giving birth after the full nine month, but when a life leaves your body, it doesn't do it quietly. The roars that left me were not because of contractions or the pains of birth, they were the pain of death. The pain of the end of a life, the end of a dream.

The first time I thought the roars came from outside me, as if it were a sound from the planet, like thunder or a volcano, but it was me. And then the young doctor would come back with a dish and not think to say, "Would you like to see your baby?" I grabbed Pete's arm, "Get it, tell him to give me my baby." That was when I saw it, my poor small thing, recognizably human, curled up and covered in blood. I did not know then to say. I want to take it home, to bury it. I did not think to ask if it was a boy or a girl.

This baby in the box must have been older than ours; it looked more complete, but not quite done. When I saw the tears pouring down Pete's face, my silent crying became loud sobs. I was used to crying alone but to see him cry broke my heart. We had learnt that to mourn our babies privately, even from each other, was the only way to bear it. If we cried together we would then cry for ourselves and each other and we were not sure that we would survive that. But now with this little stranger, who must have been in our house all the years we have lived here, must have been under our bed when our babies were conceived and when they began to die, we could no longer contain it.

Exhausted from crying, we climbed onto the bed, pushed the rubbish onto the floor and curled up. Pete carefully put the box between us and we went to sleep. I knew that in the morning the world would change again and probably become even more strange. We would have to ring the police, but for tonight, just once in our lives we would sleep with a baby between us.

Joy, Interrupted

Concerning Respiration
by Chris Reid

I remember green paint peeling from the wall I leaned against

In the hospital stairwell where I stood calling my office

To say I would not be coming to work because my child was dying

Through closed glass doors I could still hear his voice

Echo down the corridor from Pediatric Intensive Care

The sounds of his delirium before he faded away to coma

I remember what I was thinking as I looked down at him in his bed

I remember thinking nobody this sick ever gets well again

Recalling those thoughts I wonder if by thinking them I caused him to fail

When the code was called a deluge of nurses and doctors

Seemed to sprout up from the linoleum or materialize out from the wallboard

Rushing to start up the ventilator (a heroic life-saving measure)

I remember night chasing day in that elastic quality of time

Peculiar to hospital settings wherein it simultaneously

Contracts and expands much like you'd see in films

I moved through it all - through the traffic in the parking lot

The lines in the cafeteria - the clouds of antiseptic solutions

The continual distant thrumming that may have come from men or machines

I remember holding my son's hand after I was told that the mind

Whilst unconscious can still hear our world off in the distance

Chiding him to wake up it's time for school wake up we have to go home now

I wondered if cosmic forces holding me would tell me it's time to wake up

From this particular nightmare but they never manifested themselves

I thought this must be the last sensation you experience before you drown

I remember specialists queued amidst chirping monitors

The contrast of my civilian bewilderment to their neurosurgical lexicon

12

An Anthology on Motherhood and Loss

I thought I have to remember to breathe as if my own breath could keep him going

I found a Bible in the ICU lounge the probable remnant of some mother's vigil

Thumbing through the Book of Psalms I sank into the sticky vinyl chair

With a paper cup of coffee just getting colder

I remember when the waiting was over as defined by the statutes of this state

Two days of no brain function mark life's end - sign these papers here and here and here

Then the ventilator will go away - your son will go away too

Part of me was holding out for another option The Movie of the Week on Hallmark Channel option

The option that triumphs over insurmountable odds and then I signed and sealed the fate of my son

My child who tethered me to the future with each breath that he no longer took

I remember the name of the pathologist who performed the autopsy on my boy

I asked him what I needed and dreaded to know *Did I kill my son with the stroke of a pen*

But Dr. Van Dyke (named like that artist) said *No, He was gone when he quit breathing on his own*

It is about at this point that memory fails - the funeral becoming an elongated blur

A jumble of Hebrew and automobiles slowly shuffling to the edge of Oak Ridge

I think I saw the rabbi weeping over the grave but by then I had nothing more to give

13

Joy, Interrupted

The Dining Hall
by Margaret Kramar

I don't even recognize him when I arrive on campus. My own kid, working in the dining hall. Somehow I sail right past him.

Now I stand before a handsome young man, his eyes masked by the visor of his black cap. In this theatre of dancing flames, something familiar comes into clear focus: I recognize my child's hands.

He glances up with those greenish eyes, those eyes framed by dark lashes. His amazement melts into a smile.

"How did you get here?"

The word forms in my throat for a full five seconds.

"Walked," I answer.

After dinner, I huddle on a cool stone bench as the May evening loses the light. Tomorrow I'm taking Benjamin home for the summer. The new dining hall looms in the distance across an expanse of lawn. The last time I passed by this bench was nine months ago, August, the beginning of Benjamin's sophomore year.

Benjamin and I had walked toward smoking grills and tables of food, a welcome back picnic for returning students.

"Now, Mom, when we get there, I don't want to sit by you," Benjamin said, charging ahead as I struggled to keep up.

We waited in a long line of people dressed in vivid summer colors. Benjamin gazed past them, searching for somebody he knew.

I couldn't hear all of his words when he met a curly-haired kid wearing a chain around his neck. They laughed. Benjamin was happy. That's how it should be.

"Just one piece, please," I said to a student carving a roast under a canopy, as I juggled my paper plate, plastic utensils, and slippery cold can of Coke.

Benjamin left me to join a group of students in the shade of the new dining hall. A boy with wire-rimmed glasses gestured with his hands while clutching a roll. Obviously a very bright kid, a character. I wondered what it would be like to be his mother.

Lowering myself down, dutifully away from Benjamin, I balanced my plate and beverage. The plastic knife wouldn't cut through the meat, and the boiled potatoes tasted like cool rocks. I was having trouble swallowing them.

Years ago, when Benjamin was about five, we attempted to play hide and seek.

"Now, Benjamin, I'll hide first, somewhere in the house, and you're supposed to come find me."

He stared up at me with his green eyes under dark lashes, saying nothing. He started to follow.

I ducked into the sun-room, past the fireplace mantel, leaving him in the kitchen.

The silence lasted two beats before I heard a piercing wail.

"Mom! Mom!" he sobbed.

So much for hide and seek. In kindergarten he couldn't tolerate being out of my sight for even a few seconds. Now in college, he was sitting off over there.

I carved harder on the obstinate meat and choked down a raw carrot.

Benjamin! Benjamin! I cried inwardly.

At least the sun was out. Bringing him back for sophomore year wasn't as bad as taking him to college for the first time. Then as we drove on the interstate, iron droplets pelted the car windows. Benjamin stared ahead into the grey nothingness.

14

We found his dormitory and dragged his belongings down the hallway. A clean-shaven student with short hair extended his hand to Benjamin.

"Hi. I'm Dan Smith, the resident advisor for this floor. And you are?"

"Ben, Ben Dodd," Benjamin broke into a smile as he pumped his hand.

"Benjamin, it's Benjamin Dodd," I interrupted, but the resident advisor didn't seem to hear.

"I also attend a Bible study group every Wednesday and you're free to join us," Dan continued.

"No, I don't think I'll take you up on that," Benjamin said, shifting his weight to the other foot.

"But Benjamin will be attending church," I quickly intoned.

He turned around and faced me squarely.

"Mom, I'm on my own now and will do what I decide. You just have to face that."

His harsh green eyes flashed resistance.

Walking past the bulletin board tacked with notices, I crumbled, not because of his comments, but because I saw my reflection in a glass door. Who was that middle-aged woman?

Freshman orientation progressed to an upstairs room adjacent to the new dining hall. Even though we had spent months filling out reams of forms, there were more, such as a form that would allow a college representative to accompany Benjamin to a hospital emergency room if he attempted suicide. Otherwise, due to confidentiality statutes, no one would ever know.

In the dining hall, a crowd carrying trays milled around the food islands. I startled as flames jumped up on my left. From a fiendish brick oven, a boy with a white chef hat delivered what he could to hungry people longing for a tiny slice of cheese pizza. All I knew was that I didn't know this place, and I was losing Benjamin.

I recognized a woman from a summer party. She glided across the floor with her tray.

"I'm very impressed. The college personnel have been lovely to us this morning," she said.

"I hate this dining hall," I barked to her over the noise.

We located a table, but had to go back for the ketchup, mustard, drinks, couldn't find anything. Benjamin's younger siblings knocked over beverages. After years of lunches, beginning with his high chair smeared in spaghetti sauce, this would be our last meal together for a long time. I wanted to be his mother, to feel the bond between us, to caress him with affection that falls down softly like leaves.

He glared at me over his shoulder, his steel grey eyes allowing no admittance.

"Mom, you're acting weird. I'm at college now. This is the way it is. You can't face it."

His hand rested on the steel chrome structure of the chair, unflinching, marking our distance. Things were at a standstill. I couldn't let him go.

Until today, Benjamin and I were caught in the vortex of his childhood, rocking and singing in his nursery room with glowing night lights. Then junior and senior high zipped by, we argued about his college admission essay, and now we were here, his first day of college.

I remembered being back in high school, struggling with the last questions on the college entrance tests, and how the monitor blew the whistle. Stop. You must stop now. Should I have pushed him to make more friends? Stop. Did I bake birthday cakes he will remember? Stop. Does he know I did the best I could? You must stop now.

After lunch in the new dining hall, the parents sat in an auditorium, addressed by college officials. A woman with platinum blonde hair raised her hand.

"What is the college doing to prevent date rape?" she asked.

Date rape? It would never be my kid, lady. But how could I communicate this to her, and would she understand, because wasn't this a strange place, even if you graduated from here, considering that you drive up in the morning together as a family and drive home in the evening without your child?

After the lectures in the auditorium, the parents filed out onto the lawn and saw their children. Saw them, but at a distance. All the incoming freshmen were playing some kind of a game. They sat in huge circles on the grass, and then two jumped up, one chasing the other around the perimeter.

I scanned my eyes for Benjamin and, having found him, sat down heavily on the stone bench.

Other parents lingered on the sidelines, watching. They could have been interesting people, but this was no time for conversation. A pretty woman wrapped herself in a sweater and wistfulness. She only had eyes for her child. Her questions, all the years, I could only guess at the memories emanating from that sadness.

Stop. You must stop. All of these parents, up until now so busy with carpooling and coaching soccer teams, suddenly had nothing to do but watch and wait.

After the games, the incoming freshmen walked toward the dining hall in small groups, chattering with their new friends. They didn't look back at their parents, and then they were gone.

I closed the passenger car door. I shut out the grey sky when I covered my face with my hands, and sobbed all the way to Des Moines.

On this May morning, I wait while Benjamin takes his last final. In front of the student union, a wooden platform awaits graduation ceremonies. I stare at the raised planks in horror. Benjamin's only a sophomore.

He'll probably go to graduate school, get married and perhaps make me a grandmother. He may even move far away. But now I'm taking him home, with the summer stretching before us.

He'll be my boy again, for a while.

16

Departure for College
by G. Karen Lockett Warinsky

They are departing, to Baltimore,
to Denver,
to a college in Florida.

The last few weeks
spent in a nightly clench
of good times,
secret wine and
sleep outs.
Nightwalks.

The cell phones have messaged
in a flow of checking in
and arranging to get there,
to be together to have
one last cup of coffee,
one last swim,
one last chat.
They know this time is ending
and it scares them.

It infuriates the one left behind.

Community College was **NOT** part of her plan.
She feels cheated, betrayed, foiled.
She doesn't care about finances,
or reasons why,
or apologies from weary parents.
A year is **not** a ***SHORT TIME***.
All offers to ***MAKE IT BETTER***
with train trips
or plane trips
or laptops
go unheard.
She is a red, angry sore,
hot to touch
wanting no touching.
No hugging.
No kiss on the cheek from Betrayers.

The mother remembers another day...
two children,
recent acquaintances,
a boy and a girl,
both five (so wonderful to be five),
one tassel-headed,

17

one pig-tailed.

Through the window she saw them
running together
on the hill by the house,
streaming through the trees,
fairy feet on dry leaves.
Building a "fort."

Later, they were laughing on the top bunk,
laughing like they had always known each other,
these small, elfin children.
It was a perfect moment.
A perfect friendship,
and she saw.

Anirvan: The Deathless One
by Anindita Chatterjee

I woke up in a state of daze. The anesthetic effect was still there. There was a dull numbness that fuddled my brain. I could not remember where I was and what had happened to me. I saw nothing but the green curtains and the white washed walls around me. There was a picture of Mother Mary on the wall. I could not see anyone else in the room. I realized I was lying on a small bed. My hands were paining and my head felt so heavy that I could barely lift it. Suddenly I saw a woman dressed in white apron walk into the room. I looked at her and tried to lift my head. A stern voice rebuked me, "Lie down. Don't move." I didn't have the strength to ask any questions, although I wished to know so many things. Gathering my strength with much effort, I faintly inquired, "Where am I?"

The nurse in white apron told me briefly that I had been hospitalized last night due to an emergency. She informed me that I was lying in a private cabin inside the female ward of a nursing home. I could hear voices; it was getting fainter and fainter. I felt I was slipping into unconsciousness. I tried to think but I could not hold my senses together. My head was aching and my eyes were closing down. I heard the nurse's sharp voice again, "You should just lie down quietly. You have just been out of the operating theatre."

I flinched at the last two words. I wondered what had happened to me. I remembered some blurred images, my husband's faint voice, something crashing, but nothing was clear. I tried to think. I feared that the anxiety and tension would kill me. I sensed a pain and wetness inside my private parts and an uncomfortable nausea accompanying my bodily uneasiness. I wanted to see my husband, but I had no clue where he was. I asked the nurse. She said, "He was here all the while, maybe he has gone down to meet the doctor."

I waited for him to come back. Those few seconds were the most painful moments of my life. I heard the clock ticking inside the room. Mother Mary looked at me quietly from the wall. I don't know why but I was afraid. I desperately wanted to see my mother. But she could never come to me. It has been four years since Ma had gone. I craved for her gentle touch, her softness, remembered the faint smell of spices that came from her when she came out of the kitchen. I wanted to lie down on her lap the way I did when I was a child. I wanted to run and hide my face inside her, the way I did when I was afraid of dark.

I had lost my father when I was a child. I have only vague memories of him. Ma and I lived through the pain of his absence together. She was the fortress of strength that stood firm beside me and helped me grow. She taught me to be strong and independent. She wanted me to live while transcending the pain of loss. She inspired me to take every challenge in life, and live life to the fullest. "You have only one life, dear," she used to say.

The day when I found out about her terminal cancer I was shattered. There was nothing I could do to prevent the inevitable. I saw worsen every day. Weak from therapies, with a scarf worn around her head to hide her rapid hair loss, she sat on her bed and smiled at me. We had been living with each other for years. How I could survive without her? I sat with her for hours at day's end and heard her speaking softly and gently. I didn't know what to say. I just felt her words. I could not cry before her, for she had taught me to be firm. I looked at her thin white hands. I saw the pain hidden in her eyes. Women who are forced to live without their husband's support in their lives somehow gather the strength, courage and mental toughness to face the world. Ma had learnt to be patient for me, even till the last day she was there, and she tried to behave as if nothing had happened to her.

Ma had passed away in her sleep. I still remember that day as if it was yesterday. She could not endure more pain. I remember how doctors told me in the morning that Ma was gone. I kept on asking them to do something to bring her back to life. I desperately held her

19

hand hoping some miracle would revive her. But nothing happened. Her fingers didn't move any more.

It was raining badly as we cremated her. I could not cry aloud for pain had choked my throat and throttled my voice.

I thought life would come to a standstill after she had gone but, to my surprise, it didn't. I got married to Rajat after two years. Rajat taught me a new meaning of life. Rajat is full of life and energy like a bustling stream. His effusiveness found its home in my silence and tranquility.

Ever since Rajat and I discovered we were going to have a baby, Rajat's joy knew no bounds. It's been sixteen weeks and five days the baby has been growing inside me. An ecstatic Rajat proclaimed one evening, "I'm sure, we will have a boy. I can feel the vibes. We will call him Anirvan: Anirvan, the deathless one." When I had asked him, what if the baby turns out to be a girl, Rajat replied, "Then we will have to find a new name for her." I laughed at his madness. I knew he was still a child at heart.

It was October and the festive Puja spirit was everywhere. Durgapuja in Bengal marks the homecoming of the Mother Goddess. Rajat and I decided to offer Puja and take a drive along the highway. I was initially skeptical about the idea, but Rajat assured me everything would be fine. On the way back I started feeling dizzy and sick. The road conditions were bad and there was huge traffic. It started to rain as we continued to drive along the highway. Stranded in the traffic I was feeling nauseous and sick. Rajat tried his best to jostle through the congested streets. Something was bothering me inside.

When Rajat finally managed to reach home, I was feeling too weak to climb the stairs. The last thing I remember is that I stepped out of the car. It became dark thereafter. I could hear Rajat's voice calling me from far. I could not see anything anymore. Everything became dark in front of my eyes. I could not hear anything else.

When I woke up, I found myself in the hospital. I think I must have fainted. I saw Rajat's face near me. I didn't see when he had come inside the room. I could sense that something had happened to Rajat. There were dark circles under his eyes. His eyes were red. He was gently holding my hands. They had pushed some injections on my right hand and there was a pain that lingered. Rajat looked into my eyes. I asked, "What has happened to me? How is the baby?" Rajat didn't look at me this time. "You fell down. I had to rush you to the hospital." Rajat stopped. Silence prevailed. I waited for Rajat to continue.

An ultrasonography was done. The doctor saw the reports and said that the foetal pole had probably ruptured due to the fall. He was afraid that "the accident might have injured the foetus permanently. Such accidents happen at times. However it doesn't mean you cannot have a baby again."

I understood the meaning of the final sentence. I didn't have words to reply. I felt an empty hollowness inside me. Rajat told me that I had undergone a miscarriage. I realized that I had lost my first child a few minutes ago.

"Anirvan is not dead," Rajat's voice continued to console me. "Don't you remember what I had said?" Anirvan is the deathless one, he cannot perish or die. Maybe Mother Durga will bring him back when she comes home next year. I heard the sound of the *dhaks* from the distance. I remember how I cried as a child when I saw how they immersed the huge idols in water every year on the day of *Dashami*, the last day of the Durgapuja, when the mother goddess bids farewell to her earthly home with a promise to return the next year. My Ma used to tell me that Durga had to go back to her home so that she could come back next year. However, when I had immersed my mother's ashes in the water, she never came back to me.

I thought about so many more meaningless things in those few seconds of silence. Nothing seemed important to me except that my baby was dead. The journey of the live foetus inside my uterus was over after sixteen weeks and six days of pregnancy.

Rajat sat beside me telling me how there was always space for hope and life in God's world. I did not follow his words completely. I wanted to ask many questions to God himself. I did not know why God had ordained me to go through so many trials in life. I remembered my Ma used to say that God did it to see how we could be stronger, for the sweetest tree had to bear the maximum stones. Ma's words used to alleviate my fears and anxieties.

I looked at Rajat. I could hear his unspoken words. I didn't feel like talking but felt the warmth of his words soothing me in the silence of the room.

I touched his hand. Rajat tightly clasped his fingers around my hand. We did not speak. The silence said it all.

Joy, Interrupted

Voices (February 2009)
by Ruth Krongold

We climb the hospital stairs,
Avoiding chairs,
      Walking round
           And round
                And round.

She, smacking veins, drinking water,
My bruised and dearest daughter,
Until the blood vessels can be found
And pierced.

Tight flesh on faces guarding squishy innards
Witnesses stare into the vacant space between
Health and illness,
Life and death.
Mournful eyes see nothing without,
And everything within.
Deafening sighs and whispers vibrate in the hush.
Voices scream inside heads
Stories spin frantically in silence.
Bald heads.
Brilliant scarves and hats,
Immovable wigs,
Blue veined heads,
Soft, fuzzy hair on skulls,
And wafting onto pillows.
Gleaming poles with plastic bags
Swish swishing,
Dripping poison,
The menace and the cure,
Beeping endlessly.
"A single drop will burn your flesh,
to the bone.
A single drop
escaped from your veins
will kill you," says the nurse.
So they say...

Can we help	PLEASE
What can we do	LISTEN
Things happen for a reason	REASON?
Be grateful	*That my child lives*
This is a good kind of cancer	CANCER IS NEVER GOOD
Be positive	OF COURSE!
Attitude is so important	ALAS
She'll be fine; you'll see	I CLOSE MY EYES

We often see in young women a mediastinal mass OFTEN?
We don't know why RANDOM
Aggressive tumors respond well to poison WE ARE GRATEFUL
The universe has a plan GOD LAUGHS
Keep hope alive HOPE LEAVES LAST
This too will pass GAM ZEH YA'AVOR

Joy, Interrupted

Struck by Lightning
by Liz Dolan

In cruel April this eight pound Christmas baby
still lies on the sage green couch, oxygen
seeping into his lungs through a canula,
gasping as though he is breathing glass.
There are days I wonder
if he will still be lying there fully grown
like Mrs. Mac Illmurray's daughter whom I visited
as a child in their fourth floor walk up.

She, lying on the couch, shrouded
by an army surplus blanket, never spoke and stared
directly ahead at the nocturnal painting
of Christ Watching over the City of Jerusalem.
Nauseated by the smell of sweat and cod liver oil,
I relished digging my jagged nails into the jellied flesh
of her freckled upper arm, pinching her and telling her
she was faking because she didn't want to divide fractions
or help her mother dry the dishes. She never flinched. Did I learn
she had been struck by lightning or did I make it up?
Now all I can think is "Christmas is a time of miracles"
as I listen to the hiss whir of the baby's ventilator.
Already pneumonia has scarred his lungs
and now they babble about tracheotomies,
laser shavings, and Amoxicillin.
A lightning strike might take him home.

Celebrity News
by Sheila Hageman

How to capture Marc now with words.
He's alone, red-faced, scruffy in a large room.
Only Thomas and I are here.

Brother Bill visited from Michigan on Saturday.
Brother Chris chooses to wait until Marc dies to visit.
He's upset about my plans for cremation rather than a proper
Catholic burial. But then he calls and says whatever
I choose is what Marc would have wanted.

Marc twitches his nose and his bushy mustache lurches—
the most "him" thing left. That, and the lift of creases in his forehead.
And the small pursing of his chapped lips. His throat clears
and coughs still hold his sound, too.

Thomas has hiccups. "People were looking for *Scream*
this weekend at the box office," says TV. Why do we want
to scare ourselves when life already provides the horror?

And more of Lindsay Lohan's ongoing drama of jail and rehab.
This is news we care about. Not my stepfather dying of cancer,
unknown by most. Even I like celebrity news—flipping back
on my iPhone from Perez Hilton to TMZ. I crave
the nonsense; the non-scream.

Joy, Interrupted

Smoothening the Crumples: Poetry Dancing on Paper through "Kumina"
by Ann Mathew

Edward Kamau Braithwaite is wildly playful with genre and form, language and grammar, the future and nostalgia, tittering on the edges of sanity and singing the lullaby of loss in his poem "Kumina." The pendulum in the poem swings between reticence and exuberance when the woman in the poem wails for the loss of her son.

The poem begins with an explanation of the dance form, Kumina, and its movement, its purpose, and the faith embodied in every twist, turn and bobbing of the body – all which seem like an invitation to the readers, who are tourists in this particular culture and society. The first section is an excerpt from a Jamaican journal, thus beginning the experimentation with various forms. There is a foreboding before the poem begins – a brooding melancholy, grossness, distress, loss and helplessness which are all purged out by this dance form. The preparation needed for Kumina is physical, emotional and spiritual as the possession of the *myal* is an experience that is vibrant, flaring with energy and belief, with a "singing, dancing and drumming" not until the bodies are exhausted but until the spirit that inhabits them leaves this ritualistic performance. Poetry begins to thump here and we see a shift in genre. Thus, the tourist who sees the 'spectacle' is discouraged from participating or disturbing the order of things, as is apparent in the following portion:

> The cosmology of sudden unXpecting disaster
> & its unutterable grief unvomiting the world
>
> i seem to be becoming lightning rod
> for like this wreck of Time
>
> we cope so tentative so desperate in dis kingdom
> of the dread. the voices reach-
> ing out. be-
> traying fear & crying out for help beyonn the lyme
>
> of reassurance (9-17).

Once this is made clear, the speaker eludes all sense of language and reason, ushering a sorrow indescribable with the death of DreamChad's son Mark ("sun" used, either as a pun or to challenge language). The overflow of words begins and DreamChad laments for her Mark. Lost in grief so much that she cannot be consoled by her daughter Ingrid and not even by her husband. The only one who is able to stick close to DreamChad is Kamau, the writer of this poem. This overflow signifies much because, in this time of turmoil and heartache, art helps this sorrowing mother to recuperate. She indulges herself in a different world because, next, the reader finds that the genre shifts again from poetry to diary entries.

The days are numbered and the mother painfully records her activities, her thoughts, and her psyche tediously. Numbness fills in her life and makes way for her to lose her sanity too. The line: "i sit here in this chair trying to unravel Time so that it wouldn't happen twine" (45) is poignant in this observation because she wants to let go, yet she holds tight to those memories that will constantly pain her. On the second and third day, flesh, urine and blood occupy the first signs of grossness in this poem. The fourth and fifth days show a longing of the mother for the child to return to her – a child who has lost his way but who will find his mother because she is calling out to him. The description of a young white rooster is

26

interesting because it shows a belief that her son has probably returned "'home," but in another physical body which refuses to leave because finding this grieving mother is equivalent to finding its own mother. This imagery of using an animal instead of a boy is disturbing because, somehow, one feels the order of things has been upset. The sixth day is a silence that permeates through the house; the silence that the petals of the flowers sing is unique dirges for only the dead. Braithwaite plays with the notions of eternity and afterlife.

Now, the seventh to the ninth day past, the restless rivers and the inconsolable dreams show something amiss is to the mother. A heart wrenching portion is when the mother speaks: "it is my pain it is my privilege. it is my own torn flesh torn fresh/o let me comfort us my chile. is not yr heart is broken" (86). The oneness in spirit and heart the mother has lost is not only of the child but of herself altogether. A part of her responds from this time forth, only when she tries to console herself by consoling her child, who is in the pain of separation. The apparent irony is in that the child may feel no pain and grief, yet the mother believes that the life after death is painful just as death is in life when each has lost a part of themselves.

On the tenth day, the whole feeling of the language changes, becomes colloquial as more painful memories are described. She begins to crack under the whip of the memories of the unexplained murder of her child whose death is not investigated because they are a coloured race. This introduces an important issue that their country faces – racism. It pricks the viewer's heart to see that this child is simply one of those unaccounted deaths. The "No One kno" (93) is a cynical comment aimed at the judiciary for being unjust and partial and also sarcasm at God for his omniscience and omnipresence. The faith that the mother has been holding for long is corrupted and she doubts: "now i will haffe doubt if god is good & black & honesty/ wha good god do fe me?"(110)

On the thirteenth day, Mark is buried and the episode is captured with an essence of pain and agony, as more information is let in on the child's death with the description of Mark's physical self as an aberration – "skull crack. neck broken. trauma. red red red" (157). The stanza in italics that occur immediately after is a skilful commentary on the social system that Braithwaite writes of. Sung in a song-like manner, the unheard melody haunts us and throws light upon the deceitful men who only care to fill their pockets. The ones who pay the price are this mother and child – two human lives simply wasted. The poem focuses on infinite opportunities for interpretation of discourses within the medley of this music and dance. From this point forth, the unleashing power of DreamChad towards the slope of degradation is evident and the womb which bore her Mark has turned to a tomb.

The seventeenth day is composed of a very beautiful poem-song-dance that straightens the creases of the whole poem. As the pages of the book of her life turns, she knows that the title of the chapter towards the end is death. Unfortunately, she desires for this last chapter even before half the book is over. While the *"passage of tomorrow & tomorrow & tomorrow"* (197) takes charge of her daily life, her child who personifies death stands before this mother. The eighteenth day from the day of the death of the mother's beloved child, Mark, is the most important to a mother's life (as the font of the words for this day is bolder) because her child was born into this world and she is trying to keep her mind intact which can be read by her use of the symbols "<<<<" and ">>>>>" (229).

The repetition of the words "no rest" in "something inside here tell me there will be no rest no rest no rest no rest no rest no rest" (248) drum in the readers' ears. And the twenty-first day turns out to be that of a particular temperament. She remarkably accepts her saddest plight of the death of her son, but in her mind's eye travelling through time, into the future and not the time of the past, she sees and meets her son and both embrace in their forlorn beings. She fights to take him home, but realizes that time is so cruel that it has allowed Mark into her life, who has forever been blotted with the pain of a broken skull and a terror in his eyes that can never be wiped away. The mother captures this essence and soothes the child in her lullaby. She reassures and comforts the child of her presence and comes to terms with grief and pain by placing herself at that moment of time where she has reassured her child of her presence, being there in his pain and affliction. She is his Saviour. She has promised this to him while she has helped him crossover in peace. Her story has now smoothed all the crumples of a confused paper. She has danced, exhorted and sung into every inch of the page. The mother has sung, the dancers are engaged in kumina, and the tourists, with their silent pry of eyes on this spectacle, sound and movement have established one thing – that art has the capacity to engage the grievous to healing, change distress to hope and give a testimony that will forever be propagated.

Time is a constant theme that is challenged through the poem. Either there is no time, as is evident with the full stops and bars in between lines, or there is an upbeat rhythm throughout and unstoppable words that incessantly flow, unleashing words bit by bit and word by word. The brokenness of heart, the palpitations of the mother, is one that can be identified with the homeland of Braithwaite – West Indies, with a heart yearning to tell a story, kumina being the best form as the poet himself describes it through an exceptional accomplishment of exhibiting a motherly side in this poem. The deluge of homelessness, the pain of separation and the feeling of alienation have been brilliantly encapsulated by Braithwaite in this poem, "Kumina," and one can find true emancipation and comfort through this poem, that pulls together loose strings and knits it all together to reconcile two worlds of the self and the lost other.

Trinkets
by Lottie Corley

Heaven took mama in '84

We looked at each other and opened her door.

Trinkets of love throughout the years.

My sisters and I broke into tears.

Lockets of hair and baby barrettes.

Among all the trinkets that she had kept.

Handmade jewelry for her birthday.

And bright colored cards that we had made.

So much life for you to live.

So much love for you to give.

You don't get a mother's day.

Or the joy of watching our children play.

So many memories fill my mind.

So many memories in so little time.

So much love for you to give.

And oh what a life that you had lived.

A mother, a teacher and so much more.

A guardian angel at our door.

Trinkets of love throughout the years.

And showing us how to face our fears

Good-bye mama we miss you so.

And it's just so hard to let you go.

Trinkets of love you kept through the years.

And wiping away all of our tears.

Joy, Interrupted

The Sign
by Rebecca Manning

On most days my drive home from work is routine, almost mundane. I'm at the controls, but it feels pre-programmed, a sort of mental autopilot. "How many times," I wonder, "have I driven home with no conscious awareness at all?" The pattern, Monday through Friday, is always the same; the only variable is the amount of traffic slowing my progress. This is urban constipation at its finest. Today's stop and go drive is more stop than go, leaving me at the same intersection for several light changes. Red, yellow, green, wait… Red, yellow, green, wait… Over and over again, barely creeping forward with each repetition.

I pull myself into some minimum level of post-work alertness, wondering how many more inches I might move in the next half hour. Then I notice her out of the corner of my eye. I hadn't seen her at first. No wonder – there's nothing about her immediate appearance that seems out of place, not enough to draw my attention, or anyone else's for that matter. This corner is, after all, always bustling with random strangers gathered in a herd, jockeying for position at the bus stop just a few feet away.

Her long, brown, braided hair hangs neatly down her back. The occasional burst of air from a passing car makes her light t-shirt and khaki shorts flap like banners in the breeze. She's a human statue, moving only ever so slightly to shift her weight, left foot to right foot and then back again. As her body turns a little in my direction, I notice the sign in her hands.

Crudely fashioned from a paper flyer pasted over a piece of ripped cardboard, it looks like every other sign we see and ignore on street corners. But, let's be honest. Even if we take the time to sneak a peek at the sign, we never make eye contact with the sign holder. To see the sign holder would force us to admit a shared humanity – and that is just too uncomfortable. The signs always say something like "will work for food" or "anything helps, God bless." The cynic in me believes there's a company out there somewhere manufacturing these signs for just such occasions, just like greeting cards; but not today. Only after I see beyond the sign, to the woman clutching the sign, do I fully grasp the urgency and desperation staring back at me.

Her tired eyes are bloodshot and circled dark with worry – signs of endless tears. Her knuckles are white from gripping the sign tightly. She knows this cardboard life preserver is her last hold on life. But she is still drowning in sorrow. My eyes focus deeper as I see, for the first time, the picture taped below the words, written in red magic marker.

A little girl smiles at me from the photo – a smile as bright and carefree as a summer day. Her hair is brown and long, just like the woman's. I can almost hear this radiant little girl with an infectious smile giggling joyful delight, secure in her mother's love as she relishes each day's adventure. But the agony of the woman standing before me explodes in my brain, cruelly silencing the little girl's laughter. The distance from the photo to this street corner – and the painful loss that brought her here – is beyond all measure.

Somehow I know, even before I read the words. I know the message. I know the pain and agony. I know the fear and desperation. The sign reads "Have you seen this child?" Suddenly, a lump in my throat makes it hard to swallow and tears sting the corners of my eyes, running down my cheeks. I can't stop myself from being pulled into a flood of emotions. For a fleeting moment I see my own children, my daughters. The cardboard mirror exposes my worst fear as a mother. It has been said that to lose a child is to lose a piece of yourself.

I believe that the bond between a mother and her children is primal, instinctive, and even intuitive. My girls are the very heart and soul of my being. There isn't anything within my power that I wouldn't do for them or to protect them. I would fight for them to the end. If they were hurting, I would comfort them as long as they needed. And if they were lost, I would never rest until they were found.

So, I understand what would make a woman desperate enough to pursue any and every means possible, endure unpleasant or difficult circumstances, and possibly face ridicule and skepticism, in order to go to the ends of the earth, if necessary, for the sake of her children.

I know all of this as only a mother does, but I still cannot begin to comprehend the torrent of anguish washing through this woman. In a dismal sea, she is sinking before me, weighed down by grief. Her head is barely above water and it is all she can do to stay afloat with the little hope she has left. I see the weary expression and wonder how much longer she can fight against the odds. The odds are not good. I have never come close to the sense of heartache that she is experiencing. I never want to.

My mind momentarily switches gears as I selfishly think about what the evening has in store for me at home. Dinner, dishes, noisy, boisterous children, complaints about homework and going to bed, bring an unexpected smile to my face. I am suddenly filled with an extreme anticipation I haven't been conscious of in months. I am ecstatic, and at the same time wrapped in a cloak of guilt and shame over this sensation.

The blast of a car horn from behind snaps me mentally back to the reality of traffic and circumstances where I first saw her. It occurs to me that I am helpless. I offer nothing. I have nothing to offer. I watch her face peering into every passing car, searching for hope, or maybe answers, and find nothing. She will be here every day until she has found what was lost. I would be. No matter what I tell myself, we aren't that different. Desperate determination is all she has left with her ragged sign.

Finally, after what seems like an eternity, I pass through the intersection. Her eyes catch mine and hold me for a moment. Her head nods but only slightly in my direction, and I, in turn, return the gesture. There is nothing else to say or do. But pray. And hope I never see her again.

Joy, Interrupted

Dandelion Child
by Carol Alexander

The mothers
with their ashen
eyes and hands
have passed her
like a dented bead
along a snarly thread--

a rope, a towline,
its fraying end
tangled in duckweed.

The girl with knotted hair
and slippery feet
scoots on her haunches
down to water's edge,
clutching stem, crown,
a pinch of spore.

Fragments lure her--
water snake head
shiny link chain
tender pink sole
damselfly wing

and also:
susurrations of menace--
wasps nesting
plink plink of rumor
shuffle of papers
rasp of zipper.

Last one to the pond
reeks of rot and ruin.

A smell so putrid
is, the child thinks,
solid as tusk and bone
(pond muck
rat droppings
dripping diaper)
as blackened tooth
prised from jaw
against the howling pain.

Touch? Ah, touch:

Smear of bruise
stab of curse
silent pinch
tear of flesh.

The child, bands of sunburn
down her peeling back,
the scars of cigarettes
on the reticulated spine,

notes the quiet
revolution
in the earth,
and half recalls
the rules, rude and sly.
But Lilia and Marie
have fled the pond,
clambering from the
ooze, shrieking gaily,
eluding phantasmal foes.

Just one arrives
too late in the game
and shrugs: no wonder,
where rift and wrack
of cloud in coming night
glow, lurid as arsonist's fire.

Pursing plum of lips
she puffs and everywhere,
spores of nascent desire
parachute, funnel into dream,
and waft, pray, conspire
to foster in some compact
and fertile tract of soil.

Joy, Interrupted

The Cardboard Robots
by Valean Iolanda

In an embalmed spring, the destiny wove a new stage of my life. I never knew that a dramatic event was going to be seconded by a source of happiness. This sufferance-joy tandem, governs our entire life.

I was sitting on a chair in the Intensive Therapy salon of Central Hospital and I was listening to how they rhythmically inter-weaved, the song of the rain with the sounds of the artificial breathing device.

I was holding Dan by the hand, my 5 years little boy who had been diagnosed two years ago of asthma. He had had some easy attacks of asthma in those two years, but the last attack degenerated in a serious respiratory insufficiency ending with the impossibility of breathing alone; that's why he was on assisted artificial respiration with the help of a ventilation device.

I was looking at the child, with my eyes full of tears, while his feeble chest was filling with air introduced by the device. He was a good child who understood he was different from other children and was accepting his disease with resignation.

The ventilation tube wasn't permitting him to speak, but we understood each other by signs; when he was raising his little hand I had to aspirate his mouth with a special probe that was collecting saliva. Often he took the probe from my hand and aspirated his accumulated secretions by himself.

It had already passed two days from the hospitalization and Dan's condition was improving.

The doctors disconnected him from the device for a couple of minutes, allowing him to breathe alone; but after a while the little child was making signs to reconnect him, because the effort of breathing alone was too big.

For me, in those days, the outside world and time lost their sense.

Everything that mattered was Dan and his life.

Only after five days was Dan was disconnected from the device and was helped to breathe with the oxygen mask. His first question was:

"Am I okay now, Mommy?" I did not answer right away because the tears were suppressing my words. Happiness took over both of us.

Doctor Dema, who looked after us, got close to the little patient and kissed him on his forehead. Dan hugged the doctor and asked him happily:

"Can I have some tubes to play with?"

"Of course, young man I will bring you many colored probes," said the doctor, excited by the child's request.

"Thank you," said Dan, enjoying the doctor's acceptance.

I stood up, looked in Doctor Dema's eyes and thanked him for all his care.

"Thank you, for giving him a new chance to continue his life."

The doctor was thinking, but after a short hesitation he took me by the arm and he led me outside the salon.

We continued the dialogue on the corridor:

"I don't want to scare you, but there is the possibility for such severe asthma attacks to repeat in the future too. When you will notice the symptoms are worse, you will have to present yourself at any medical emergency service."

"And one more thing, do not travel with him in places that do not have a hospital. In any moment he may need special medical care," said the doctor, worried.

34

"I will be very careful with his condition, besides I also suspected these kinds of hard episodes could repeat," I said to the doctor with the trembling voice.

The doctor took my hand and told me on a serious tone:

"I am convinced that you know in what a difficult situation you are in …" With a final effort of not collapsing I answered:

"I know, Doctor, that I have a child with serious health problems, but I assure you that I am living only for him."

"I see that Dan is in good hands," said the doctor, and he left to another salon, being used to such hard situations.

After this discussion, I returned to the salon beside Dan, who, although he didn't hear anything of what we had spoken about, was getting sad seeing my face tensed. I took him in my arms and kissed him on the cheeks. Suddenly, he asked me in a thick voice, because the lesions on the vocal cords made by the ventilation tube:

"Mum, after we get out from the hospital I want to make a robot from cigarette boxes."

"But, where do we get so many boxes?" I asked him curiously.

"The doctor smokes many cigarettes. I will ask him to give me all the boxes."

"When we will come for checking we will bring the robot to the doctor too, okay?"

We both laughed at this extraordinary idea.

It was evening and Dan had fallen asleep; it was the first night when he was sleeping without the device. In that night, I didn't even sleep a minute because I watched his breath. We both were facing the biggest challenge of our life.

In the morning, suddenly the door of the salon opened and a team of doctors and nurses entered with a stretcher and a girl on it who was making huge efforts of breathing alone. I shuddered; the symptoms were the same as Dan's.

In a few seconds the little girl was intubated and assisted by the ventilation device. Her lips were purple.

I was standing in the middle of the salon and I was watching, useless, at the little patient and I didn't understand why these children have to suffer from this disease.

For two hours the medical staff was beside the girl until her condition was stabilized.

Unlike Dan, the girl was unconscious at the arrival and she even suffered respiratory arrest and was resuscitated successfully.

In the door of the salon a man was sitting and holding a doll in his hands, watching with concern what was happening.

The emergency doctor was getting near him and told him:

"Go home, the girl is safe and her condition is improved."

"Doctor, I will not move from here until you let her go, if she will stay alive," said the man, determined.

"Okay, you may stay with her, but when medical maneuvers are made, you have to leave the salon," the doctor replied.

"I will obey all your rules, but keep my girl alive," said the man while he was reaching for the doctor.

The man slowly got near the unconscious girl's bed and put the doll beside her. He was standing motionless, looking at her without blinking.

Understanding his suffering, I got close to him and told him:

"Calm down, the girl will be okay. My boy went through similar moments and now he is feeling well, thanks to the medical team."

He looked at me surprised, then looked at Dan and still remained quiet. I continued to encourage him because I knew what he feels in his soul.

"If you need help I am permanently here," I told him.

He hardly mumbled:

"Thank you."

I withdrew beside Dan, seeing that the stranger from the salon wanted to be left alone with his suffering.

The sick girl was motionless in bed beside her doll.

All night long the nurses and the doctors administrated her perfusions and drugs.

In the morning, Dan woke up and asked the man who was holding the girl by the hand:

"Is your girl sick as I am?"

The man hurried to answer:

"Yes, my girl is very sick."

"She is going to be okay. I was very sick too," said the little guy.

I stood up and went to see the girl who was in bed motionless. The man came close to me and reached his hand and presented himself:

"I am sorry that I wasn't communicative with you but I am desperate because of my girl. My name is Marian and my girl's name is Sena."

"Nice to meet you, I am Elena and I am Dan's mother."

"Dan suffers from asthma, too?" asked the man, curious.

"Yes, he suffers for some years of this disease, but we are used to this condition," I answered with the hope that I could calm down the man who was standing helpless beside the girl's bed.

"I see. Sena had some minor asthma attacks, but now I don't know what happened to her," Sena's father continued with trembling voice.

"If you are tired, you can go home and you can send your wife. I am not moving from here, I am staying permanently beside Dan."

The man looked at his girl and with a voice, fainted by the pain, said shortly: "My wife left us when Sena was one year old and exactly a week after she left, the girl had the first asthma attack. I cannot tell you what moments I had lived then, when I was alone in the world with a sick girl."

I couldn't believe that in front of me was a man who lived the same drama that I did a few years ago, when my husband left both of us. In that moment the words were hurrying to come out from me, like a release of the pain accumulated in time.

"I am sorry that you endured hard moments. I understand your situation, I went through something like that as well. Dan's father left us and settled in another country. Since then, I haven't got any answers for the multitude of questions which my son addresses me regarding his unexpected departure."

We were silent, gazed at each other and felt an affective bridge form between us.

Marian interrupted the silence, changing the subject:

"If something has to be bought from outside, I shall be responsible for the supply."

"Marian, do you go to buy cigarettes?" asked Dan rising from the bed.

Marian looked at me, questioning. I explained Dan's plans of building a robot from empty cigarettes boxes. He was excited by the little guy's idea.

"Dan, I do not smoke, but I have a lot of smoking friends, so I will bring you many boxes and you will build an army of robots," said the man with a sparkle of joy in his eyes.

"Mommy, did you hear what Marian said?" said Dan jumping in the bed.

"Yes, my dear but try not to agitate yourself, stay calm in bed, robot time will come, but now you have to get well."

"Mommy, can I get out of bed and go beside the sick girl?" asked the little guy.

"Yes, you can go, but be careful at the tubes of the device, don't you break anything."

Dan gets near Sena and he easily takes her by the hand. The girl had no reaction, she was inert. Sena's father was looking at her.

"Mommy, why isn't Sena waking up?"

"She has to rest so she can fight the disease," I explained the child. "Now go back in bed, don't get tired too much."

From the doctor's reaction I found out that Sena was in a critical state. Her father quickly understood that her situation was serious, because the respiratory arrest that she suffered affected her brain. The reanimation doctor approached again to Marian and explained to him that the girl's condition was critical. He left the salon, restraining his sobs.

After some minutes, I heard him screaming out of pain in the yard of the hospital. I went downstairs after him and I held him. It was such a natural gesture, which I would probably have never done, but in those moments he needed support. Instinctively, Marian held me in his strong arms and he was crying without stopping. I felt that I was breathless but I stood still until his pain decreased in intensity. His pain was confusing with my pain. His tears were flowing on my locks of hair. When he exhausted all his tears, he released me, apologizing for his weakness.

"I am sorry, but I don't think that I will be able to live without my girl."

"She is going to be okay, but she needs time to recover," I encouraged him.

"She won't recover, the doctor told me clearly that she is decerebrated, that means she has no normal brain activity because of the respiratory arrest that she suffered."

My thought ran to Dan and I immediately realized that anytime it could happen to him too.

I started to cry as well, this time he was trying to calm me down.

When we returned to the salon, we both had the sensation that we were spiritually emptied.

A deep silence occurred. I was standing beside Dan's bed and he was holding Sena's doll in his arms and he was watching how his girl was fighting to stay alive.

"You know what hurts me the most?" he asked me.

I looked at him desperate without even been able to answer his question.

"My helplessness in front of the destiny, I thought that I am able to do anything, even to move the mountains, but it is not like that, I am a simple mortal vulnerable in front of the blows of life."

"I am here for you, you can count on me," I strongly answered.

"Thank you, you inspire in me a lot of trust."

In a couple of hours he didn't want to communicate with anybody, he was motionless beside Sena.

Two more days of agony passed and the girl's condition did not improve. Dan and I were sent home, he was feeling well. I said goodbye to Marian, he hugged me again with strength and I promised him that I will come to see him daily at the hospital.

For a month I went to see both of them daily. His despair was bigger, he was devastated.

One morning when I went to the hospital, I saw him on the stairs of the hospital staring. He didn't wave to me and he didn't speak to me.

I ran into the salon and I saw the empty bed. Sena died a few hours ago. I started to cry without stopping. A nurse came and took me in the emergency room. I couldn't understand how Sena was wronged in her short life.

I left the section and went to Marian. He hugged me again and told me:

"I was a helpless father."

"That's not true. Probably Sena had to go on another trip."

"What will happen to me, I don't want to live without her anymore."

"Come to our place, stay there as much as you want. My company and Dan's will help you."

Marian looked at me surprised and he accepted without hesitating my invitation.

From that moment on, for both of us, started a new chapter of life. He remained beside me and Dan, we fell crazy in love, and soon we became a fulfilled family.

At one year after Sena's death, Marian told me the most beautiful sentence that I had ever heard in my life.

"I want to build a Centre for the children with respiratory diseases."

All my being was filled with a huge happiness. I looked at Dan who was looking at Marian questioning.

"Your idea is brilliant," I exclaimed, excited. "I will support you in accomplishing this project."

"Mom, what does project means?" Dan asked me.

We both started to laugh at him and we explained him:

"When we had built together the robot of cigarettes boxes that means we made a project of what you had in mind."

"I see," said the child.

"I was thinking, to do the same as you, but I won't build a robot, but a big house where sick children who, like you, sick of asthma and other diseases, will play," Marian explained to Dan with a paternal tone.

"Will you make a real big house, or will you make it of cigarette boxes?" asked Dan.

"No, my dear I will build a house like the house we are living in," said Marian.

"Will I play with the children too?"

"Of course, you will be their boss," said Marian laughing.

"I can't wait to play with many children," shouted Dan happily.

"You are a special man, I am glad that you entered our life," I told Marian who was already concerned with starting the first sketches.

"I will build this center in the memory of Sena and for the children who have these respiratory sufferings. If I will succeed, I will be finally professionally fulfilled."

"Together we will succeed in making wonderful things," I answered the man who gave brightness to my life.

"I know, thanks to you I recovered my lust for life and the joy of making well for people. I already thought about the name of the center … the center shall be called: 'SENADAN.'"

"You are magnificent," I answered with joy.

"I combined the name of my two children," said Marian sad.

From that day, we began to start the project of our life.

Marian had some real estate and by profession he is an architect. He sold all that he had and designed and built a modern center for children with respiratory diseases. The name of the center remained – SENADAN.

We are both spending our days working at "SENADAN" with a lot of children, who are engaged in different interesting activities – games, creation competitions. Each child is received in the community after he builds a robot of cigarette boxes.

In each room there are medical personnel, inhalers and aerosol ready to intervene when the children need.

The entrance is guarded by lots of cardboard robots, made by children who frequent this heavenly sanctuary.

The cardboard robot is the symbol of the centre.

Joy, Interrupted

Cluttered
by Sheila Hageman

Thinking about my next memoir—
the Uncle Tommy story
at a play-space birthday party for Genny's friend.
Nursing in a Technicolor room; my natural fleshy rounds against
rainbow blow up slides and broken whack-a-moles.
Blasts of *I'm a loser baby so why*
don't you kill me—
as six-year-olds dance.

Yesterday at Barry's office—
big mahogany desk with legal files stacked,
Hong Kong book and his business cards.
I'm Peggy's POA now, too;
she jokes not to commit her.
The cottage reduced in price;
the Anna B for sale now, too.

I volunteer to clean my grandparents' house—
to save Tommy: his stuff, my memory.

When will I be able to let go
of everyone and their stuff?

Star Bunk
by Anna Steen

"I see the Big Dipper, and Orion's Belt, and Cassiopeia. Do you see them?"

"Yes," I whisper, eyes closed.

"Imagine a black sky that goes on forever. There is no end. And although you know there is no end, you try to find it."

"I'm imagining it."

"It's hard to imagine, but try."

I open my eyes in the dark room and four feet above me are the stars, attached to my son's bedroom ceiling, glowing with a plastic power I don't know or care to understand. From his top bunk of the bunk bed, we are high and tall, as if in a tree. Cuddled together like two monkeys high atop for protection, no one else in the world to bother us. The warm, stuffy air surrounds us, blankets us, and I feel so safe up with him I consider staying here all night.

Classical guitar drifts through the air and, when I close my eyes, I see the player composing each line just for my son and me as we lay curled in his bed minutes before he falls asleep. I have these melodies memorized. The notes drift out of the stereo over the art-desk, overflowing with paintings and drawings, down to the floor where a miniature city of Lego's sits. The princess is safe in her a makeshift space station with the mismatched Lego men thrown around her. It is a room I could not have imagined six years ago, but now have memorized and cherish like a glass trinket I can open and crawl into.

It is past his bedtime now, I know. The sky is dark behind his constellation curtains, and the real stars he rarely sees are just now appearing. He moves closer and I stroke his arm. I cuddle with no one like I cuddle with my son. My son can have his face pressed next to my cheek, squeezed under the nook of my arm, live there for hours. I would never take this from anyone else. I need my space. But I'll take him morphing back into me. As if he understands he was once part of my skin.

I lean over to kiss my son goodnight on the cheek before I climb down. He kisses me back. For him, kisses need to be equal and, although I cherish every kiss from him and never want this to stop, I want to teach him that love and kisses do not have to be equal and measured. But at five, I will take every kiss.

Joy, Interrupted

Still-Life: Embracing the 2009 Void
by Danelle

"We don't hear a heartbeat. Get the doctor."

All day, the baby had been giving me problems. Earlier Thursday morning, I had visited the gynecologist who had to dig deep into my city slicker to find her. She was turning herself to the side, a horizontal acrobat. His hypothesis, she was kicking and might break my water that evening. He was right, of course, but she was contorting herself as she was choking to death. My first mistake was choosing an obstetrician gynecologist who didn't have an ultrasound machine in his office. He visualized kickball, while the child was playing Twister. The second mistake was not asking him to break the water that minute. I certainly was ready to deliver and be delivered. I was on the verge of gestational diabetes and had developed a foul smelling white patch of yeast underneath my armpit as my sweating reached epidemic proportions. At that time, it would have been the water of life, not the brackish waters of mortality. With a clueless grin, the doctor sent me on my way and indicated that if the baby didn't break the water, he would induce labor on Monday morning.

In the meantime, Samantha died. Around 8:30 pm, the contractions began. I was excited. I walked about fifteen laps around the swimming pool not only to get my mind off the pain, but I prayed the waters would break instead of dive into the abyss that would actually take place.

Samantha had not been planned. I had been working at museums in Washington DC, broken up with my fiancé and ended up in the arms of a professional alcoholic. His drinking was so severe that I would find bottles of liquor in the trunk of our cars. He would fail to remember our Capitol Hill dinners and conversations with friends that took place two or three days prior. After six months, I had to eject him from our apartment. Life seemed to have balanced itself out. I was single again, over the rebound stage and looking for work at local colleges to teach Art History. Unfortunately, my monthly gift from the gods didn't arrive and I was in the confessional at St. Patrick's Church with Fr. Sal faster than you can say Unplanned Parenthood.

I whispered. "Forgive me Father, for I have sinned. It's been two weeks since my last confession."

"Yes, my child."

I don't know why I bothered going into the confessional. I knew he recognized my voice and would see the darkness underneath the screen. The church had two black members including myself and the other was an eighty-five year old man with a hunchback.

"Well, remember all the fornication sinning you said you were tired of hearing about. I'm pregnant and because I don't want the relationship Stephen doesn't want me to keep it."

I let Stephen aka Sammy Sosa back into our home for about a month, but it was unsuccessful. After every argument, he made it a point to throw his drafting instruments and brushes at the artworks on our walls. At one point, I even slipped on a Sunflowers print of Van Gogh's and began to bleed. The bleeding eventually stopped as did my patience for him. I decided to name the baby Samantha based on his pitching skills. He left the next day.

The priest practically toppled his chair and seemed to want to throw it in a rage. Thank goodness I was behind the screen. He roared:

"Don't you know you're a hero? Keep your baby."

His words affected me deeply, not only because it reminded me of an Enrique Iglesias song, or because I feared for my life, like the traders at the temple, but who wants a pro-life black woman. Certainly not society. Black single mothers are perceived as menaces to society, raising wild black sons who may endanger the lives of the middle class or, better yet, end up in altercations at Urban Beach weekend in Miami, FL during Memorial Day Weekend.

So, Samantha and I traveled to Miami, FL where I found a part-time college teaching gig. Of course, I didn't mention the pregnancy in the interview. They assumed that I was overweight and I provided no edification. By the third week, my boss knew I was pregnant but I already had my job. The students were at my mercy, image after image, of mother and child. I had been abandoned by the decency of her father, but not her spiritual father in heaven. So it became a Madonna and Child Art History festival from Duccio to Chris Ofili. The students were blessed with images of sacred motherhood and awaiting mine to feel some brown relief from my holy feminist lectures.

At 11:00 pm, my wail was a long and wet one. I remember the long drool which emanated from my dry, cracked lips. I knew that she was gone. The kicking stopped but the contractions did not. I had to vaginally deliver a dead baby, swaddled in serpentine twists. The pain was beyond excruciating, with no help from the silent one. Each futile push led me closer to a ripped vagina and finally, faithful forceps were used to pull her from my still womb on Friday at 1:24 am. The seven and half pound sleeping beauty was bathed and placed in my tired arms. Her father was racially mixed, half African-American and half Caucasian with blue eyes. I could not resist. I had to see if she had inherited his intoxicating gaze. Samantha's eyes were tightly closed and I pushed them open with my quivering fingers. Her lifeless black eyes stared blankly at me, asking me why I attempted to retrieve her from the river Styx. She was gone. And so I embraced the void.

The class never saw a Madonna and Child the remaining semester. Not one mentioned a word about her death. One student, Maria, could not find a babysitter one evening, and brought her baby girl to class in a soft, pink blanket. The baby made very little noise. At first, I wanted to be incensed. This is a college level course. What is she doing bringing this creature into my class, but she had no babysitter. I was teaching at a community college, Maria worked two jobs, had no husband, and promised it would not happen again. Holy feminism was being tested as was my faith.

I had kept this child, why had she been taken away? My spiritual father failed to answer this question and in retaliation, the students were bombarded with the works of Yves Klein and everything that has been written about his works. My special emphasis was on The Void. Instead of an empty gallery, my students were forced to enter my nothingness, my barren beliefs and disloyal womb. The priest had entered my hospital tomb but did not baptize my dead child. How could he? I had very little to say to him and to her as well. I did let her know that she was my best friend. Not only did I birth a lifeless child but a damned soul? I didn't want to consider the implications or ask the Indian Catholic priest as I saw him tearing with sadness. I had gone through the preparation for motherhood, but did not get to enjoy its fruits. I was a Pieta before I began.

I have begun to explore the Buddhist concept of the void. It is a concrete experience and in my case, it is a container of her ashes and the dust of my faith.

Furies

Be near me when the sensuous frame
Is racked with pangs that conquer trust;
And Time, a maniac scattering dust
And Life, a Fury slinging flame.

Lord Alfred Tennyson, "In Memoriam A.H.H"

"Unknown Hero" – Mark Moore - Arcylic

Joy Interrupted

After our daughter died, my husband wrote an angry letter to God. Part of the reason he did so was because he needed someone to blame. The determination of SIDS as a cause of death really undermines the ability to blame anyone or anything other than God, the universe, or some other ultimate being. But, I think he also wrote the letter because he needed something to do. It's this action that I think defines anger and what I think makes it the opposite of depression, when you feel too helpless to do anything. I think you also feel helpless when you are angry, but this helplessness often translates into furious action without a specific or constructive purpose. I see this furious action in Monika Pant's "Run..."; action that may in fact be pointless, but what else can we do?

I like the visual of anger being a type of fury. In Greek mythology, the furies were three goddesses who acted out of vengeance and had no mercy. Unlike the typical goddess, they were horrible to look at with snakes in their hair and blood dripping from their eyes. Grief can be raw and harsh, as I expressed in my piece, "Blow by Blow," and as I saw in Gabriella Burman's "Push Pull" and Nina Bennett's "Sound Effects."

I also like that the furies were protective, advocating for those who could not do so themselves; they had the ability to make things right when human laws could not. I close the section with Kim Hensley Owens' piece, "On Being Lucky, And Not," because we can be "furies" regarding the existential injustices of others. Many times, as in the case of Sandra Kolankiewicz's "The Proud Parents," we have to be furies to protect our own children.

I wouldn't be furious for years until after my daughter died. This is probably true of many mothers who have lost a child because of the way many women are socialized. We are much more likely to feel depressed, guilt, or be angry at ourselves. I open the section with Liz Dolan's "Andrea Yates, Swim Team Captain" because it felt like the most obvious exposition of fury turned inward-- and then out.

I chose some of the pieces in the "Furies" section because they elicited this sense of fury in myself. I felt the fury in Margaret Kramar's "The Soap Opera," Lisa Wendell's "Hiatus," and Robyn Parnell's "Maddie is Dead," all of which gave me permission to feel angry while grieving.

I found it easier to feel angry when there an injustice, or something that seemed out of the order of how I think life should be, that happened to *someone else*. I felt this type of anger when reading, Trangđài Glassey-Trầnguyễn's "pumping anonymous" and Alan Nolan's "Mother with Cancer."

Reading the pieces gave me permission to feel angry, and the guilt, the inwards anger I had carried for years, began to dissipate. I felt some anger dissipate while reading Trangđài Glassey-Trầnguyễn's "If you can't wake up at 3am to feed your infant, don't release your sperms."

I know that for others, like my husband, feeling angry comes naturally. And maybe such individuals would have entirely different reactions to the pieces in this section. But, I think recognizing the furies in loss, no matter your level of comfort, allows you to see how we strive to rise from the ashes. Our movements, our efforts, might be pointless for quite awhile after a loss, but the "furies" keep us going, nonetheless.

An Anthology on Motherhood and Loss

Andrea Yates, Swim Team Captain, Valedictorian
by Liz Dolan

Train up your child *in the way he should go*
so when he is old he will not depart from it.
                                                  Proverbs 22:6

I imagine Andrea, struggling
to keep her boys still
as they squirm and giggle in the third pew
with Mary nesting,
a gosling by her heart. Next to them
her starched-shirt husband
eyes shut in meditation.

Then I see Paul, Luke, John
and yearned-for Mary, lying
pale as Beleek under sheets.
Eight eyes wide open.

Noah, seven, still
floats in the tub, a tuft
of Andrea's hair clutched
in his fist. His last gasp,
I'm sorry. Andrea did it
to save their souls; *they did things*
God didn't like: chewed too much taffy,
tossed Tinker Toys hither and yon, forsook naps.

Her nails encrusted with their jellied flesh,
she felt at once a wicked mother
and the sweet relief of a fabulous
relay back-stroker who passes
the baton to a mate without looking.

Joy Interrupted

The Soap Opera
by Margaret Kramar

When Spenser was born, the doctors spoke in muted tones. The relatives didn't know what to say. With their helium balloons sagging around their shoulders, they painted smiles on their faces while in the hospital room, then turned and walked down the hallway of the maternity ward, their heels clicking on the linoleum, trailing tears.

My Spenser was not born a healthy baby, and the doctors in white coats wanted answers. I didn't want my child to be labeled, and resented their wheel-of-fortune diagnoses.

Sotos syndrome. Marfan syndrome. Fragile X. They scribbled notes in their charts, slapped them shut and left to make their rounds. I stayed behind in the room, eyes downcast.

Of course I was in denial. I expected a normal child. A thin, wizened baby with a gastronasal tube took his place.

On a windy but sunny day in late February, my sister and I descended the grey concrete steps in the parking garage of KU Med Center, carefully balancing tiny sleeping Spenser in his car seat. The wind blew against the glass, and as we scurried across the street to the main building, white paper scraps flew wildly around the curbs. We had an appointment with Dr. R. Neil Schimke, division director of endocrinology, metabolism and genetics.

Dr. Schimke, a tall man with thinning grey hair, leaned against the examining table in his white coat.

"So were there any complications during the pregnancy?" he asked, arms folded across his chest.

"No, none at all. This was totally unsuspected."

"Any problems or complications with the delivery?" He looked at me through his glasses.

"I pushed for three hours, and then I had to have a C-section."

"Hmmm," he tapped the pencil against the chart. "Were you exposed to any toxic substances?

"I cleaned the oven, but held my breath every time I sprayed the fumes," I said.

He asked all the routine questions I had heard in other medical offices, trying to crack the code of why this wasted little wraith lay before us in his blue knitted jacket and grey car seat instead of a fat, squawking thing.

Really, there was nothing. My sister, still wearing her parka with the fake fur ruff, pulled the requested family pictures out of a manila envelope, to discover if whatever Spenser had was stealthily slipped into the gene pool.

The three of us gathered around the black and white images arranged on a metallic table. Did our grandfather have a long face and large skull? Did our father have an unusually large forehead? Once beloved pictures now looked sinister. All were suspect in the relentless investigation of this perfect crime.

Spenser slept with his eyelids sealed, oblivious to all the apprehension surrounding him.

"He's not always this quiet. From about two to four in the morning I'm pacing the floor with him," I said.

"They're perverse that way," Dr. Schimke chuckled.

I did not share all the secrets of what transpired late at night, when I awoke to his muffled cries and pulled my heavy body, still disabled by the cesarean section wound, down the stairs to his crib. In night's blackness, I could not see the bruised face, but could feel his skull against my forearm, and smelled the fetid aroma of urine evaporating from his damp

48

sleeper. Spenser cried, but would not feed. When I positioned him to accept my nipple, he squirmed, but would not latch on. He then cried weakly while I walked through dark rooms with the moon shining in from the crescent window, my bare feet treading on cool wooden floors. Finally, still hungry, Spenser would get quiet, and I would lay him down on the crisp white sheet and pull the coverlet trimmed with lace over his thin body. Within days my breasts, initially tender and bursting with milk, dried up without a trace.

Dr. Schimke, grasping the edges of the yellow tape measure between his thumb and forefinger, measured the distance between Spenser's two pupils. The black notches formed a track bridging his nose.

Dr. Schimke looked up at the nurse. The moment had come. Without speaking, she carried the baby out of the room, and Dr. Schimke followed, so that he could do more measurements, and come up with a verdict.

"Sotos syndrome." I looked up to see a doctor who was decisive, but carefully handled the fragility and power of the truth. For me, having any diagnosis was shattering. I had prayed that this doctor would assure me that my infant was normal.

"What does that mean?" I blurted out. Dr. Schimke's lips started moving, and his eyes lit up as one conversing. I heard maybe every eighth or ninth word, sometimes single words, sometimes a group of them. Big hands, big feet, may be clumsy, large head, advanced bone age, possibility of cognitive developmental delay, of developmental delay, developmental delay.

"Does that mean he's going to be mentally retarded?" I shrieked. Dr. Schimke's head and shoulders were outlined in stark relief against the white wall. I had no more defenses. Outside a brown shriveled leaf blew down the alley.

"It's too early to know with certainty." Dr. Schimke answered.

There would be many subsequent late nights, the household asleep, when I sat in the garret overlooking thick woods, reading, praying and journaling. Let him be normal, let Spenser be a typically-developing child, please God. But underneath the supplications was an aching chill. I ran from the truth, but whenever I looked over my shoulder it was there, like an elfin ogre with gleaming teeth, peering out from the pages of a fairy tale.

Mothers have universally thought that this couldn't be my baby, no, not my baby. With his large broad forehead, slightly slanted eyes and small, pointed chin, Spenser physically resembled E.T., the space alien character from the movie. He was an extraterrestrial, who had come from some far off planet to dwell on earth.

A few days later, I sat in the television room with Spenser's hard skull pressing my forearm against the wooden arm of the chair. The voices of soap opera characters made the only sound in the house. A manila envelope arrived from KU Med Center, with a letter that stated, "After examining him we feel that there is a possibility that he has a condition called Sotos syndrome. Clinical features involve a large head, large hands and feet, advanced bone age, and a variety of other problems some of which are described on the enclosed information." I didn't want to read this, didn't want to read this.

The letter continued, "Occasionally, children with this condition have developmental delay, however, this is not a definite feature."

Enclosed with the letter were pictures of babies diagnosed with Sotos syndrome. Naked except for diapers, rectangular black boxes blocked out their eyes. I read the captions under the pictures. This baby, with a winning smile, had an IQ of 60, that one, propped up on weak legs, 70.

"How can they know? These are just babies!" I yelled at the television screen. Spenser slept, and I studied his still features for symptoms, such as premature eruption of teeth. With my forefinger I shoved aside his lip to examine the smooth pink gums, finding a little white blotch on the gum ridge. A tooth.

My hopes drained swiftly out of me and spilled all over the floor. Spenser had Sotos syndrome. This clinched it. I didn't even have the energy to rock, to make the hinges in the stiff chair squeak.

I heard the front door swing open. Steve, my husband, wearing his tie and jacket, took one look at me and Spenser and froze. He stood before the picture window in its afternoon light.

I lifted the manila envelope from the telephone stand, and dropped it.

"They sent some information about Sotos syndrome. I think from reading this that Spenser has it."

Steve stared at me through the metal rims of his glasses.

"What does this mean? Is that baby retarded? Is one of us going to have to quit our jobs to stay home with him all of the time?" he demanded.

I sat there. I couldn't get up.

During most of the early afternoons, when Spenser was taking his nap, I couldn't get much of anything done. When Spenser woke up, I rocked him, and watched soap operas.

One day one of the actresses was giving birth. With her coiffed hair only slightly mussed and the slits of her eyes delicately lined under iridescent dark lids, she tossed slightly and emitted noises from a lipsticked mouth that formed a circle. Of course it was a normal, healthy baby.

I hated the actress simulating birth, absolutely despised her. I not only raged at this woman, but also the screenwriters, for never even daring to imagine an alternative outcome.

Run...
by Monika Pant

(Dedicated to the Tsunami victims)

Run...run anywhere...
Hold your Papa's hand and run...
Don't scream little baby, hold me tight.
I wish I had more arms to hold you tighter.
Run...just run...don't look back...
The water's chasing us, run faster than the water...
I didn't take my savings, my daughter's trophies, my husband's certificates...
Run... now... faster…this time the water's up to the knees.
Don't fall little child, don't hold my ankles, I can't bend down...
Leave me ...my daughter's drifted away, I must go back...
She is crying... I can see her hand raised
I have to swim...no... she can't swim...
No...don't pull me on...I have to go back...
I won't be pulled to safety while my daughter's carried away
There's a boy gasping for breath, let me save him...
Maybe someone else will save my daughter.
I had to buy a gift for my husband's birthday,
I promised a tricycle to my daughter.
I can't see her anymore.
...I have to go on...to save my other baby
The water's up to my head now, it's pulling at my baby
No...no...not again, let me die instead.
Don't go away, dear husband, I had pledged to live and die with you.
I can't live alone, alone...alone...in the swirling, sucking waters,
I was so happy yesterday...
In my little two-roomed flat, I did not ask God for more,
Or, maybe just a little more…look what he's giving me...
What was that which bit me…I hope it doesn't bite my children.
Let it carry me...maybe... then it will spare my babies.
I didn't know the sea was so big, it'll scare my babies.
Take me ... along, to where they are...
I can't look anymore, my eyes are hurting…
How will I recognize my children?
The water's in my ears now, and in my mouth.
I can't breathe...I can't see...I can't hear...
The screams anymore.
Maybe this is Death.

Joy Interrupted

Maddie is Dead
by Robyn Parnell

Dead.

Karen, how nice to run into you.

Maddie is dead.

How are you? How's Michael?

Michael's alive. Maddie is dead. I push the cart down the aisle, and Maddie is dead.

Excuse me, ma'am. Ma'am? Will that be credit or debit?

She's dead.

Heard about our special? A free car wash with any fill-up over twelve gallons.

Dead is dead. Fill 'er up; my daughter is dead.

* * *

Go to the closet. She's still dead. Chose something. Anything.

"You look nice. Green has always been your color."

Maddie is dead. I look nice.

"I'd choose a matching tie, but you said anything green close to my face makes my eyes look like peeled grapes." Michael knotted a navy blue noose around his neck. "Remember? You actually said that, once."

Maddie is dead. I will never again say anything of consequence.

"Karen?" Michael placed his hand on his wife's shoulder. "Thanks for doing this. We can leave early, if you like."

* * *

Karen lifted the cup to her nose. The neon cherry-colored punch had no aroma.

It's all dead. Maddie is dead.

She took visual inventory of the conference room: beverage tables, canapé buffets, a no-host bar, and a sinuous silhouette in a black/silver sequined dress, standing drill sergeant straight in front of French doors that opened onto a balcony. That woman had been watching Karen ever since Karen and Michael arrived at the party.

A waiter balancing a tray of champagne glasses on his upturned hand approached the punch table. Karen averted her eyes and mouthed, "No, thanks." She pretended to sip her punch, looking over the rim of her cup. That woman was still staring at her. Karen stepped backwards, gasping when the table edge jammed into her thigh.

Dead. Maddie is dead.

The sequined woman strode across the floor, her stiletto-heels clicking a purposeful *TAP-tap, TAP-tap.* A waiter carrying a tray of drinks passed behind the woman, who fluttered her hand at him. The waiter followed her to the punch table.

"Here." The woman's eyes never left Karen's as she gently pried Karen's fingers from around the punch cup. She took a glass of red wine from the waiter and gave it to Karen. She took another glass for herself, draped her left arm around Karen's shoulders and wordlessly steered her out the French doors and onto the balcony.

Dead dead dead.

"My name is Mara." Her simple words coiled like the ivy tendrils wrapped around the balcony's railing.

My name is Dead. Maddie is dead.

The woman sipped her wine, arching her neck as she swallowed. She looks like the majestic heron that hunted frogs in the creek behind our house, Karen thought. Our old house.

52

"My son died three years ago. Isaac was eight." The woman took another sip. "He collided with another boy, playing tag at recess, and collapsed on the playground. Cerebral hemorrhage. He was gone by the time we got to the emergency room."

"I'm sorry." Karen gulped. "I am so sorry."

The woman lifted her glass, as if toasting someone across the room. "Isaac had Sam's —his father's — eyes."

Karen turned around. A tall brown man in a brown suit waved to Mara.

"Isaac was all Sam around the eyes and forehead. But he had my nose and mouth." Mara looked over the balcony railing. "When Isaac went to his first sleepover we chided ourselves for being wimps. Only one night; how could we miss him so? Sam told me that whenever Isaac was gone we could simply look at each other, and between the two of us there was Isaac, looking back." A breeze wafted across the balcony. "Sam and I haven't made love in over two years."

Karen downed her wine. It was tannic, and sucked the moisture from her tongue.

"And yours?" Mara asked.

"I don't see…there." Karen spotted Michael in a far right corner of the room, holding a plate of canapés and chatting with his boss. "It just makes it worse," she heard herself say.

"When you try to tell?"

"Exactly. But if I can't say it, then there's nothing. 'How was your day; what do you want to do tonight….' Maddie was four."

"Yes."

"We named her Madeline, like the girl in the books."

"Ah," Mara murmured. "'In an old house in Paris, covered with vines, lived twelve little girls in two straight lines.'"

"She was at a birthday party, for a boy from the old neighborhood. We don't live there anymore. I don't remember moving, but Michael said we had to."

"That was probably a wise decision."

"She choked on a balloon. They think she tried to blow it up but inhaled it instead. She'd gone to another room, by herself, when the boy opened his presents. Maddie didn't like noise. She was blue when the boy's father found her. Now she's dead. She'll always be dead."

"Yes," Mara said. "She will."

Karen set her glass on the railing. "Maddie loved our garden. She made dirt igloos for worms. She smelled like rich earth under her fingernails. She smelled like a world growing."

"Mmmm, that's lovely." Mara inhaled deeply. "How long has it been?"

"Seven months."

"It won't get better. Just different. But, different is better." Mara took a silent swig of wine. "People say the word 'heal,' to my face. Ignorance doesn't intend cruelty; still, there it is."

"I haven't sold a painting in months." Karen wiped her palm across her lips. "Not even a sketch. I'm down to one gallery that still displays my work. They won't take my new portraits. They say, 'You're no cubist — where are their hands?' I can't paint hands anymore. I cannot draw a person's hands."

* * *

"There's no evidence for gods." Karen plopped down on the bed and kicked off her shoes. "But there are demons. Male, of course. They invented high heels."

Michael sat down beside her. "That's nice," he chuckled.

"Nice? My feet are killing me. That's downright wonderful."

53

"I mean, it's nice to hear you joke." Michael lightly touched the zipper on Karen's dress.

"I met someone, at the party." Karen leaned back, resting against Michael's hand. "Her husband's named Sam, do you know him?"

"Sam? Don't recognize it. He could be in accounting. What was her name?"

"Their son Isaac died three years ago. I can't remember if she told me her name."

"What did you talk about?"

"What do you think we talked about?"

Michael fingered the hem of the bedspread.

"Clover honey, dripping down the edge of a serrated knife — that's what her voice was like." Karen shook her head. "I don't know what she said. She didn't say it will get better."

"But it will." Michael's voice was flat, spongy. "I promise."

"Maddie's dead, Michael. For as long as we live, she'll be dead."

Michael shut his eyes.

"She's dead. Every morning when I wake up, she dies."

"Don't," he moaned. "Don't you think I know?"

"Every day, Michael. Every single, fucking-hell day. 'Poor Karen and Michael; they lost their daughter.' Maddie is *dead*; we never *lost* her. We knew exactly where she was."

"It was an accident," Michael whispered.

"You're not supposed to hate anyone's child, but this is necessary." Karen pulled her knees to her chest. "He had greedy fingers, snotty nose, fat teeth, and his eyes – he had a bully's eyes. The others at the party were from his daycare; none of the neighborhood kids would play with him. I felt sorry for his father, when he brought the invitation over. He'd been making the rounds and no one had said yes. Do you know why I told Maddie she should go? It was just to be kind. Know what else I told her? I told her if it got too loud she could slip away to a quiet spot and find a way to amuse herself."

"No. Oh no." Michael curled himself around Karen's feet and rubbed his nose against her ankles. "It was just a tragic, freak accident."

"I believe in freaks," Karen said, "and tragedy. But not accidents. Maddie is dead."

Michael burrowed his face in the rumpled bedspread. "I told the real estate agent we'd take the first offer, any offer," he groaned. "I thought if we stayed, I'd see him one day, playing ball in the street like any other kid, and I'd strangle him. I wouldn't be able to stop myself."

Karen held her breath and began to count. When she could count no longer she inhaled and looked down at her husband. She pressed her lips to the back of his knee. "Stay right there; don't move." She darted across the room and removed a sketchpad and a small box from the chest of drawers by the closet.

"Like that; yes...." Karen sat on the bed and touched Michael's hands, which were wrapped around the back of his head. Her arm moved in quick, light strokes, the pastel chalk between her thumb and forefinger whispering across the sketchpad.

"Just like that," she sighed.

pumping anonymous
by Trangđài Glassey-Trầnguyễn

my name is New Mother
i had a first-time C-section, unscheduled, five weeks preterm;
and my baby doesn't latch for the first two months

everyday i sit at my desk
and pump, evoking all milk ducts
to pour forth, calling on all water bodies
around the world to run in

and i pump/ i pump/ i pump
and i pump/ i pump/ i pump
and i pump/ i pump/ i pump
and i pump/
i pump

even when i hate the flanges squishing my boobs,
even when i fear the pain induced when the speed revs on, sucking my
        nipples away,
or when i doze off against the broken air in front of me,
my hands frozen from flange-clutching,
my mind electrocuted from sleep deprivation

still i pump/ i pump/ i pump
still i pump/ i pump/ i pump
still i pump/ i pump/ i pump
still i pump/
i pump

but how can i make do with the alienation of my breast?
the absence of my flesh in the bottled milk?
the instant production of packaged love?
the constant abduction of mother-child fellowship?

from the nipple to the bottle
occurs the dis-identification of the liquid gold
my body produced with the little life that it has
having gone through birth (the way i didn't want to)
and the boundless world of newborn care

how will my child and i connect through the gap between breast and
        bottle?
how do we bridge the distance of my milk,
being changed hand, when my spouse aids in the feed?
the abstraction of my lactation from human milk to merely food in a

Joy Interrupted

       bottle,
off my chest, no longer of my breast,
did nature fail me?

but if the baby latched,
would i be willing to endure the infamous nipple sore?
oh, who wouldn't?
i was, two months after birth.

Push Pull
by Gabriella Burman

I can count on one hand the number of funerals I had attended before planning the funeral of my five-year old daughter. I was the kid who held my breath in the car when we passed cemeteries. I refused to look beyond the gates. When I was sixteen, my grandfather died of cancer. The funeral was quickly held in Detroit, before his body was flown, with my father, to Israel for burial in the holy earth of Jerusalem. In my twenties, I attended the funeral of someone I did not know; his wife was my boss and it seemed like the right thing to do.

Michaela died suddenly in her sleep, on a Saturday morning in May, 2009, during a routine sleepover at my parents' house. My mother had dressed her in dainty blue pajamas with scalloped trim. My father woke the next morning to find her not breathing.

As a member of the once-priestly tribe of Israel, the kohanim, my husband, Adam, was given the choice to bury Michaela in a section of the cemetery where she would have been "surrounded by old men," he said. He declined. So early the day after her death, Adam went to the cemetery. He chose her final resting spot past a small lake, in the children's section spotted with the markers of those who lived a day, a year, or not at all.

I had been wearing the same red sweatpants and shapeless blue tank top since Friday, when Michaela had been alive. I had given birth to our third daughter, Maayan, twelve days before. Now my top was sticky with breast milk. We returned home Sunday afternoon from my parents' house to dress for the funeral. From the outside, our house looked the same. The irises were about to bloom.

Inside, the rooms had been prepared for the initial seven day mourning period by a woman from our synagogue: I imagine she quietly and reverently opened several drawers and closet doors until she found our bed linens, which she draped over and taped to the mirrors. There were, also, two black arm chairs with the legs cut off, set directly across from the couch, where, just two days before, Michaela had sat with Maayan, while I shot photographs. I don't know how anyone got the key.

Our friends from out of town seemed to materialize out of thin air. I had the perverse sensation of preparing for our wedding all over again. Many of the same faces, who had come to Detroit nine years before, were here, again. Laura and Daniella sat on my bed and helped me pick out what I would wear. But no compliments were paid. Nothing was going to fit. I was a shapeless woman who had just given birth.

All I knew is that I didn't want to wear all black. Michaela was a child, so the color did not fit her. How I had any sense of right and wrong, at that moment, is a mystery to me to this day.

We chose a long, summer dress that fit over my breasts. A babysitter arrived to help watch the nieces and nephews. I left our two-and-a-half year-old middle daughter, Ayelet, on the floor of our bedroom, watching Dora the Explorer; she would stay there for the better part of the next two weeks, her puzzles and dolls left untouched.

Joy Interrupted

My parents drove Adam and me to the funeral home. I had instinctively grabbed photographs of Michaela from the coffee table. I propped them next to the guest books: a school portrait, in which she wears a brown t-shirt with pink ribbons sewn across the front, the apples of her cheeks framed by a soft bob, and the new bangs we had recently styled for the first time. She is sitting up straight and lovely, and you'd never know she was a child who couldn't speak or walk or chew or dance, in the ways we all think of when considering these verbs.

The other photo shows Michaela on her adaptive bike, holding a baseball bat across the handlebars, wearing her cap cocked to the side. This photo was taken in 2008, when Michaela played on a team for kids with special needs, assisted by Dena, her teenage friend, from a Detroit organization that fosters friendships between able-bodied children and children with disabilities. Michaela sat strapped safely in the bike and pedaled passively, while Dena navigated her around the bases. This was our preferred method of traveling for Michaela. In a wheelchair, she would not have had to use her legs at all, and a child with limited mobility must work out her muscles all the time.

In a small, unlit room behind the sanctuary at the funeral home, we beheld Michaela's small coffin, draped in black velvet. Our parents faced us, but not to fix a corsage to my prom dress or straighten a boutonniere. In keeping with Jewish law, they tore the collars of our clothing. We would wear them that way for a week. Adam collapsed against the coffin, draping it with his long basketball arms, and cried out for his daughter.

Eventually, we, our parents, and our siblings turned from the coffin to walk out of the antechamber, and I hissed, "Don't turn your back on her!" Everyone froze, and then stepped backward out of the room, as though from the Western Wall in Jerusalem. Adam escaped into the restroom. I feared he was throwing up.

We sat in the front row. Dena and her mother sat nearby; I had asked her to read a speech about Michaela that she had given at a local fundraiser. The pews were overfilled; people lined the back wall. They made up the guest list of the bat mitzvah Michaela would not have.

*

I am writing today in the kitchen. There is too much sun. I prefer the cave of the basement, where I can dim the overhead lights, and the moon of the computer is enough. Two years on, this craving for darkness is related to our desire for sleep. As my friend Daniella told me over the phone last night, "You are too existentially tired to explore what the world has to offer."

*

She was somewhere behind me, at the funeral, clutching Laura's fingers. But I didn't look backward, as I took my seat, except to instinctively reach out my arm out to one of Michaela's physical therapists who was standing in the back. After that, I faced forward, with Adam on my left and my mother on my right. My father sat next to her, and then my sister. I think that's how we were grouped. It's possible to be wrong, and for it not to matter.

Michaela's teacher described her last day at kindergarten. Her classmates had straightened her glasses and her feet, as she stood in her pediatric gait trainer beside them in class. He said that she had transcended her difference and achieved something magical: "She belonged," he said, and then he added, "And now she is more like us than she was before," which stung as a reminder of our common mortality. Finally, he asked the rabbis if he could end with a song, "When the Rain Comes Down," by the late Bob Devlin, which is popular in elementary schools.

Michaela's teacher electrified the room. I didn't want him to slip away. In the background of the recording of the funeral you hear me moaning, "Why can't she stay in the class?"

*

Speaking of the recently deceased in the present tense is common. I recently sat with a friend whose mother died, and he told me what kind of friend and hostess "she is." Like everything else that comes lose from its mooring after a death, so, too, do subjects de-tangle from verbs; they no longer "meet," but drift apart, and then, like mismatched puzzle pieces, never quite fit together again.

*

The funeral ended. Pallbearers lifted the coffin, from its place at the front of the sanctuary, and began the slow procession to the hearse parked outside. Bewildered, I held onto Adam and followed Michaela outside. I searched for my sister Naomi, who had always tied Michaela's ponytails more neatly than I had. I gathered Naomi to me, and we exited into the blinding sun, of Memorial Day weekend, ten years almost to the day when Adam and I had first met in New York. The congregation followed us into the parking lot, lining up on either side of the drive, in order to allow the hearse to pass through. When it rolled to the end of the drive, I panicked and cried, "Where are they taking her?" The crowd surged forward to assure me that she wasn't leaving without me.

My father's Cadillac pulled up next, and Adam and I got into the backseat. A caravan of cars followed us to the cemetery, a forested place I had never been. They were, of course, expecting us. A tent had been erected over Michaela's freshly dug grave, a mound of dirt and a shovel by its side. A few chairs for the family had been set up in front of it, but only Adam and I would approach near enough to sit.

The sight of it startled me. Who digs a rectangular hole in the ground?

At first, I sat on the chair, and, then, I moved to the ground to look over the edge, as her coffin was lowered. My skirt spread out around me. I sat in the grass, until my mother coaxed me back to my chair. She held up my face between her hands. The rabbi asked us to rise to say Kaddish and ask Michaela for forgiveness. "I'm sorry for all the times I spoke to you unkindly," I cried. Dirt hit the top of the box, as people took turns covering the coffin with earth; but I can't tell you if the wind blew, or if Adam wept or groaned.

Like the Red Sea, the crowd parted ways, again, after the burial was complete, and Adam and I walked past the mourners who had loved Michaela. But we weren't headed to any promised land. Our elevated existence lay behind us, scorched away by a loveless God, who, in one stroke, had destroyed our family.

And then, in a pattern that repeats itself until this day, I was kidnapped from my grief and hurled into the land of the breathing. I had to go home. My breasts were straining against my dress. The time had come to nurse Maayan.

59

Joy Interrupted

The Proud Parents
by Sandra Kolankiewicz

At first we did not admit to them, imagined
cradle cap, skull plates still shifting into
place. Then we pretended they weren't
there, forming under our palms when we

cupped them, stretching the scalp under his
forehead, small round knobs reddened with

the effort of pushing toward the light. Next,
we covered them up under a blanket in the

sun, knitted hat against the cold, hood pulled
down, string tight at his chin. By that time,

of course, we couldn't sleep, rose through
the night to steal across the room, peer down

into the crib, fretting that they were
growing. Soon it became impossible to say

our son wasn't sprouting horns—however
we tried, especially when others would gasp

and glance away. We explained, "He really
wasn't like this yesterday," or "They are

smaller than they were before." In a while,
like others, we grew ashamed at them,

especially when they bested the size of our
thumbs, even if persons who couldn't

look at him assured: "He has such a pretty
face." We probed our own heads, acquired

jealousy at the smooth brows of strangers'
children, smarted at wordless comments,

swelled in response until, like his cranium,
we prickled. Eventually, however, though

they peeled as he developed, we began to
adore them, couldn't imagine him

protrusion less, bald, particularly when we
saw other children with projections worse

than his, shafts like unicorns in fact, waxy
and vulnerable, not nearly as attractive as

our son's horns, ultimately quite inferior. By
then, we felt sorry for parents who tried to

60

hide their offspring's crown.   Or when
people snickered, we thought: *you just wait.*

Joy Interrupted

Blow by Blow
by Melissa Miles McCarter

Maddy was born on September 1, 2003 and died on October 6, 2003. Her death certificate says CAUSE OF DEATH: SIDS. Sudden Infant Death Syndrome--also known as crib death.

My pregnancy had been one worry after another. However, it never even occurred to my husband and me that we might lose Maddy to SIDS. After her death, we tried to find some cause for her death other than the official one, which seemed almost to be a non-diagnosis. I had been taking lithium for years for bipolar disorder; Maddy was exposed to the drug the first two months I was pregnant because my HCG levels were too low to even show in a blood test that I was pregnant. I later learned that the low levels signaled that the pregnancy wasn't viable; but Maddy hung on, burrowing her way into my body and heart. We were unaware of the series of blows that we would experience.

Once I knew I was pregnant, I discontinued lithium because there was a risk it would cause congenital heart defects. On advice of my psychiatrist, I stayed on the antidepressant Celexa throughout my pregnancy, which I would later find out carries a similar risk as lithium. I also started taking the anti-seizure medication Neurontin as an alternative to lithium because it had a low risk profile. We were so careful, trying to make the best decision for my mental health and Maddy's well-being; but once she died, we second guessed every decision.

The first blow came at 16 weeks into my pregnancy. The doctor told us that according to the ultrasound, Maddy might have Down Syndrome. We had already decided that if we were to find out that she did have Down Syndrome, we would abort. We wanted a healthy baby or no baby at all. The window to abort was about to close; right before the 6 months "deadline," we found out from a specialist that the original ultrasound did not indicate Down Syndrome. It either was an error in measurement or interpretation. I thought back to the fact that a blood test failed to detect my pregnancy, and now an ultrasound had detected a phantom abnormality; I didn't know that these medical irregularities would haunt my pregnancy and Maddy's birth.

The next blow was around the corner. At the same time we knew for sure that we wanted to carry the baby to term, I began to have frequent contractions. They put me on Brethine and steroids to stop premature labor and to help develop Maddy's lungs if the drugs couldn't prevent it. I was also told that I had to be put on bed rest for two months. The Brethine made me feel like I was on speed and the steroid made me angry and irritable. So much for trying to control my moods--the medicines I was taking, to keep Maddy inside in me or healthy if she was born, caused me to have symptoms that mimicked bipolar disorder. I spent the last month of my pregnancy in bed, wanting to run around the house at high speeds and snapping at my husband.

The next blow came at the next ultrasound, about three weeks before my due date. We discovered that Maddy was in the breech position. We were so beaten down at this point, having dealt with blow after blow in the course of this pregnancy. My OB/GYN told me we could try to "turn" the baby by their manually manipulating Maddy's position in the doctor's office. We breathed a sigh of relief for a moment but then we had another blow.

I thought I was leaking amniotic fluid and went to the emergency room. The nurse monitored me for a few hours and dismissed my fears. Around this same time, my sister's ex-boyfriend committed suicide and she asked us to come with her to pay her respects to his family because they lived about a couple of hours away from us. We got the okay from the hospital to travel. We figured, outside of the family obligation, it would be one last time to have some sort of vacation before Maddy's arrival. After blow after blow, we thought it might rejuvenate us.

We left Tyler, Texas and continued on for a weekend trip to Louisiana. My husband had it in his mind that he wanted to see Kate Chopin's home in Natchitoches. Being nerdy English doctoral students, this seemed the best way to have one last hurrah. My husband's two-year old son, who was also my step-son, came with us on this final family trip while it was still just the three of us. We stopped in Shreveport, and went to a casino to have a breakfast buffet. I was at the end of my 37 weeks and we planned to return home a few days later in order to have Maddy turned, or, if this failed, for me to have a C-Section. We never got to see Kate Chopin's home.

My water broke. I had to have an emergency C-section in Shreveport, four hours away from home. We were in a small Catholic hospital where we weren't even sure our limited graduate school issued health insurance would cover. My husband stayed with my step-son and I was rushed to the operating room, all by myself. We thought that now that the pregnancy was at a definite end the blows would be over. It would all be over, and I was looking forward to holding my daughter in my arms.

Blow. Maddy was born, but she wasn't breathing. I kept asking, is she okay? But no one would tell me what was going on. Later, I would find out that they thought she was having a seizure. She was rushed into the NICU and I was brought to my room to recover from the C-section. I wouldn't get to see Maddy until the next day. **I was in agony in bed, feeling my uterus painfully shrink to its original size and wishing I could hold** my daughter in my arms.

After my dad took a picture of her with his cell phone and showed it to me, I was motivated to get up and walk around a few hours after the surgery. I had to be able to get into a wheelchair before they would take me down to the NICU. Luckily, Maddy was stable, not having had another seizure. **Because my culture tested positive for strep, they decided to keep her** in the NICU for about a week to observe her while she was on antibiotics. Every three hours I went down to try to breastfeed her, but she had trouble latching on and I wasn't producing enough milk. They supplemented with formula and I pumped in between seeing her. Even my breasts were failing us.

Three days after my surgery, even though I was officially discharged, they let us stay in our hospital room until Maddy was able to go home too. The night before we were to take Maddy home, we got to "co-room" with her. My husband held her **swaddled in a fuzzy pink blanket** and watched a football game. I held her in my arms under a LSU blanket he had bought me after wandering around Shreveport while I was recovering from surgery. We tried to breathe easy, walking out of the hospital with her after she passed the "car-seat" test, in which we proved we could safely strap her in. We were on our way back home.

While we thought the blows were over, that everything had been so worth it despite all our difficulties, I still had lurking concerns. She was born, at 5 pounds 5 ounces, a bit earlier than we wanted. I hadn't gained any weight in my pregnancy and soon was twenty pounds lighter than my weight before I got pregnant. But the worries started to wane when we went to her first pediatrician's visit and she was almost 7 pounds. I was starting to gain weight. My milk was starting to flow more easily. Maddy hardly gave us any trouble, sleeping on schedule and very rarely crying. The blows were done. Or so we thought.

The morning Maddy died, I was beside her in bed, having fallen asleep next to her after we finished breast feeding. This would soon haunt me for years. When I first looked at her, she looked like she was sleeping, content with a small puckered smile on her face, swaddled in her pink blanket. I reached towards her, about to change her diaper after our long nap, and I realized she wasn't breathing.

Joy Interrupted

I called 911 and was told to put her on a flat surface. We were taught baby CPR at the hospital, but I couldn't remember anything. I tried to suppress my panic and listened to the instructions. They told me to blow into her mouth. But her mouth was full of mucus; I couldn't get her to breathe. After one blow, a small drop of blood came out of her nose.

In my heart I knew she was dead, even as I saw them working on her and hoped I was wrong. I feared that the doctors would never get her to come back to life. The doctors took forever before they confirmed this fear, which they did when my husband was on the way to the hospital. I was the last one to see her alive. After being interviewed separately by the police, a week of funeral services and being comforted by family, and then my husband going back to work, we were left with trying to deal with life, day by day. The blows had stopped, but we were broken in the wake of Maddy's death.

I was afraid the horrible pain, feeling like I had a broken heart, would never end. For a while, I was a defective robot, unable to do the simplest tasks. I felt old before my time, unable to look forward to the next stage in life.

We thought the blows had stopped. They still come, like aftershocks.

Blow. Sometimes I feel guilty because I know that if Maddy had lived, my husband and I wouldn't have as much free time together. I feel bad when I think about how old Maddy would be now and the milestones we might be enjoying. I love spending time with my stepson, but his company often reminds me of the joy we felt when Maddy was alive.

Blow. I run into a former student of mine from when I was a graduate teaching student at the university. She had last seen me pregnant and asks, "How is your baby?" I took a moment, tried to breathe, then, said, "She died of SIDS." I didn't know how else to answer, and the conversation ended abruptly. This would be the first of many such conversations.

Blow. I walk around campus and see all the innocent, carefree students starting the new semester, and it seems their only worry is what class to take. I feel like I have a visible gaping wound. I have become "a mother whose child has died." There's no other way to describe me.

Blow. I can't let go of the day Maddy died, the last day I saw her. It is frozen in my mind, for me to go over and over, and it clouds my memories of her. I stare at the few photos we have of Maddy. I try to remember every moment I had with her. I can't get the image of her dead, lying beside me--and then my trying to revive her--out of my mind.

Blow. I have physical reminders of Maddy's gestation, and eventual birth, that I cannot avoid.

One is the scar on my belly from the C-section. This scar fascinated my stepson, who would often lift up my shirt so he could gently touch the purplish line. "Who did this, Mommyhead?" He asked. I answered, "The doctor." He looked sad. "The doctor not supposed to do that. He hurt you." I said to myself, "You're right--this shouldn't have happened."

Blow. Back then, my step-son doesn't understand where Maddy is. To him, she's just gone. Sometimes, he asks my husband where Maddy is. It pains me to see my husband have to remind his son that his daughter, my step-son's sister, is dead. Britin doesn't ask me, instead saying to me, haltingly, "Maddy is in heaven."

Blow. There's a period of time when I can't reminisce about Maddy with my husband. Any mention of her name seems to pain him. To my step-son, he only remembers seeing her in the few photos we have of her. He doesn't understand why I am sad, pointing to the picture, seeming to say, "Don't worry, Mommyhead, Maddy is right here."

Blow. Everyone who is close to me waits for me to fall apart. I am eerily calm, numb, functional, but an automaton. I only cry alone. I deadened myself, because life would not stop after Maddy died. Sometimes I wonder--if I had let myself break down, beyond a little at a time, would I feel less empty, resigned?

Blow. Sometimes, when I wake up the next day, I hope that my life will be a different story.

I never before had wanted to have a different past, to wish that life had been otherwise. I used to think, "Things might have been bad, but it was worth it to be at this point in my life." But the narrative of my life has been interrupted by Maddy's death. I have to accept that tragedies cannot be unwoven from my life. I have to accept that the blows never stop, just slow down, fading into the background, like a heartbeat I wish I could hear again.

Joy Interrupted

Sound Effects
by Nina Bennett

I didn't scream the night she died.
I wandered from one empty chamber
to the next, then back again,
repeating the process without thought;
my heart beating while hers did not.

On the one week anniversary
I tried to sing her a lullaby.
Roaring up from my toes,
molten lava burned my throat
as a wail released, a volcano
erupting into the winter night.
Propelled by grief, it reverberates
like the screech of a trapped rabbit
summoning others to its rescue.

None came.

Previously published in: The Broadkill Review, Volume 2, Issue 6 2008

Hiatus
by Lisa Wendell

When I stepped into the shower and began to feel the effects of the Seroquel, I thought, "This is your mind. It's your mind that's sick." Thirty minutes earlier I had tucked the little pink tablet at the back of my throat and washed it down with a Redtail amber ale. It was 2:30 on an eye-piercingly bright Tuesday afternoon. The air outside was thick with late autumn heat and sluggish birdsong. A day that wore a tight felt cloche. I had stayed home from work.

I prodded for thoughts of Maxx. Yes, there they were, the ever-present throb, but now the drug had tossed a soft drape over the pain. This was all I needed. Something to relax gut muscles flexed into a state of near constant internal contortion against which I was powerless to remain erect.

I can't remember the start of the lurch, but I can tell you where it took me, as always. Physically, to the crawl on hands and knees in the hallway outside his bedroom, then to the bathroom, then back to the threshold of the kitchen where the carpet meets the fake wood. That was where I had collapsed with my head bent over onto my knees, and begged him to forgive me.

"I didn't know, Maxx. I didn't know."

He had put his arms around my shoulders and helped me to stand. My gracious, loving boy with Stage IV blood cancer helping his mother to right herself and walk to the couch.

"Mom. Mom. Come on, get up. It's all right. There's nothing to forgive. You didn't do anything wrong."

But I knew that I had. There is no changing a mother's heart-shriek for her child, for what she will die knowing is the truth. I was not wise enough, or strong enough, or vigilant enough. Enough of anything to save him.

I dragged myself back and forth across the carpet in front of his closed bedroom door pulling at my hair and screaming into closed fists, the two Chihuahuas frantically licking the snot from my upper lip. Soft dog kisses. Calling for Maxx. Begging to die. Begging the emptiness. Pounding the walls. Begging to go back in time. Willing my heart to stop as fervently as I had willed his to continue.

"You made a mistake, you bastard. You took the wrong one."

I ended up in the kitchen, opening the drawer with the carving knives. There were several, but only one that was really sharp. I knew that to be effective one had to slice down hard vertically. I touched the point of the knife to the inside of my wrist and pressed the tip into skin just above the heart chakra tattoo and below the Sanskrit words for "Truth" and "Reconciliation."

"Maxx," I whispered.

I didn't see him. I didn't hear him. But I knew he was shaking his head and his eyes were filled with sadness. I placed the knife back in the drawer.

How could such powerful strength of will not be able to alter the course of events? We live in a time when belief in the power of positive thinking has become another false oracle, a god-like concept that robs us of the ability to discern spurious lies from what is real. The religion of positive thinking creates a fervor supported by anecdotal stories, mind-numbing, cult-like reverence and behavior that supports entire commercial industries, but the only truth, that which we must know and face if we are not to live as cows led to the slaughter, is that the power of the single cell, diseased, malevolent, violent in its biologically driven force to reproduce, is stronger. That is real. We may "face" our death with some kind of equanimity,

67

though that is probably bullshit as well, but we all die. Nor can we, when we choose, wish ourselves into a grave. I am proof of that.

The water hit my face and my mind began a slow softening in response to the first quiet swell of calm. I can get through, I mused, with appropriate "assistance." There were bottles of pills in the house, none of which did much for long, but sometimes a new combination was more effective than another. People lived for years on medication, didn't they? Millions of people were working, shopping, eating, doing whatever it is that I was coming to feel I could no longer manage. Millions of bereaved parents who did not kill themselves or die from broken hearts (not so easy to do apparently) who continued to fill prescriptions for sedatives, anti-depressants, sleep meds. They were in this world, not of the world perhaps, but in it nevertheless.

So then, would I be. I could not, would not end my life. So this would be my next best choice. Fuck yoga. Fuck the spiritual path. Fuck understanding and acceptance and integration and all the other crap-filled horseshit concepts of professionally and culturally accepted grief staging. I had birthed, lived with, and cherished a complicated, joyful, brilliant human who had been brutally ripped from my life in a meaningless headlong rush toward death from a cancer so vicious and cruel, it was hard to know where "then" ended and "now" began. My pain was unimaginable and if anyone deserved her prescription medications, I did.

For the next several hours I rested, and then the anxiety returned. Like clockwork. I felt my stomach assume its twist back upon itself, my mind chugging back into overdrive. There they were, flickering images of his illness, his dying, his baby days, his childhood, his smile, his eyes, his flesh, his hairline, our conversations, his laughter, his intelligence, his long "piano" fingers, the tag on his toe when he died in ICU. He took good care of his feet. He always cut his toenails. Unlike his father. I would tell him that women hate men with long dirty toenails. Cut your toenails. And he did. He flossed regularly.

These are the memories that come racing back into their ready-made grooves, powerful channels the psychiatrists claim we create with repeated thoughts, a sewer of a caustic pain. Without intent or control, mind-retching forces excavate serrated pathways deeper and deeper into the convoluted folds of gray matter that make us, each one, who we are. You would think by now that my tears would have diluted some of the toxicity that continues to poison my soul. Another lie. There is no purifying quality in tears. For me, uncontrollable crying is the signal that I must dam the flood lest I end up washed ashore like so much fly-specked rubbery seaweed.

And I will say this because so few will, and it is true and needs to be said. Thoughts of suicide are a mind-rape and they are more compelling than most are willing to admit. Given the surreal quality and the heart-walloping force of grief in what we trusted had been and would remain a "safe" life, it is no wonder that more grieving mothers don't kill themselves. In the wake of these thoughts, our eyes no longer focus in a way that reflects reality as others see it. Or, expect to see it. Vision is wavy, fluid. Nothing remains fixed. These are not hallucinations. This is a blurring down of sight. A gradual dimming. It is not that the world disappears, or that what we do visualize occurs in odd configurations of space and time. It is only that what we are capable of recognizing no longer matters.

When I stood under the shower feeling the drug bring me back from that place where no human can live for long, I realized that the only reason to go there is to die because if there is no substitute for the lost beloved in those moments when you hit bottom and understand the full meaning of where you are, the soul vanishes. Despite my agony, I needed to stay alive. I didn't know why. But I knew that I must continue to be present. And if being present meant that I must rely upon chemical support, if only to give my worm-eaten brain temporary respite from repeated grief-assaults, then that is what I would have to do.

This is it. All day I stir the sickening soup of my life. All day, I add some of this, some of that, a thought about this, a memory about that, something to make it more, or even less, palatable. Every day, I circle the edge of the cauldron and I do it with full awareness. Some days, I let it simmer, some days I stir vigorously, but always it is cooking and always I am moist from its steam, revolted by its stench. It is always full. Bone fragments, teeth, bits of hair, globules of unidentifiable matter are forever bubbling to the surface, popping and spattering, a sticky fulminating broth of obscene pain. And so I cook the stew until the moment when I must take a pill or fall forward into the burning brew.

I dwell now in the land of Over and Over. There is no circle of life here. Only the repetition of a nightmare that will not end. Where can I go? How can I live like this? What is this place without my boy?

It is two years since he was diagnosed and I watched his eyes go glassy with fear and disbelief on the exam table. "Lie down baby. Lie down." His face had drained of all color. He was already snow pale. I thought he would faint. And though I feel certain that my heart cannot take this much longer, it does. It must. I am still here. That is the way of this. Grief. I will do what is required. And I will try to stay alive. Like he did.

When I returned to work, people asked if I'd had a "nice" day off.

Did they forget that I'm almost dead?

"Fine," I answered, the edges of my brain, moth-eaten filaments, fluttered like torn gauze strips in the sigh of my words.

"Thank you."

Joy Interrupted

Symphony in E Minor
by Nina Bennett

Overture
The months of my daughter-in-law's
first pregnancy pass more quickly
for me than her. An early ultrasound
doesn't determine gender.
Midwife thinks girl,
urine DNA test purchased
online pronounces boy. My preference
isn't one of gender; secretly I hope
for a redheaded grandchild.

First Movement
The baby dances to Dave Matthews,
keeps the beat when my son talks.
For Father's Day I crawl through the attic,
find his bent hardback copies
of *Goodnight Moon* and
Where The Wild Things Are,
purchase fleece coveralls
that look like lime sherbet,
a gender-neutral color ideally suited
to red hair. My grocery cart
is taken over by disposable diapers
and tubes of Boudreaux's Butt Paste,
bought because I like the name.

Second Movement
A CD plays softly in the
yellow birthing suite, where
windows on two walls
let in the fading light of
mid-November. Labor
progresses like an orchestra tuning,
cacophony of squeals and screeches.
Unable to find her note, she seeks
the comfort of the tub.

Third Movement
She pants and blows, cheeks
puffed out in exaggerated
mimicry of the woodwind section.
Gradually the head emerges,
turns awkwardly to permit
passage of first one shoulder,
then the other,

quickly followed by the realization
the baby isn't breathing. The cadence of CPR
fills the room like a metronome—
one and two and three and still
her heart doesn't beat.

Fourth Movement
I cradle my granddaughter
warm from the womb,
kiss her red eyebrows.
My son brings his baby home
in a porcelain urn painted
with dragonflies
instead of the dark blue
safety rated car seat.
I set aside my classic rock
and listen to Mahler's Kindertotenlieder.

Joy Interrupted

If you can't wake up at 3am to feed your infant, don't release your sperms...
by Trangđài Glassey-Trầnguyễn

(In honor of my life partner, Olivier, and my new life, Kiên-Lucas)

The Grind

It was early. Always. 2am. 10am. 5pm. It was early. I couldn't wake up.

Days and nights bled into each other. When did a day end or start? Or does it even start or end? The sense of time evaporated. Everything gelled together into a whirl of consecutive/repetitive/predictive activities. I lay motionless in that whirl, meditating the piercing pain across my body.

I felt so down.

How could I? I was sunshine to the world! My friends counted on my delightful spirit to keep them alive.

How could I? I just gave birth to the most gorgeous person I had ever met! And the best part: I got to have him all to myself. I felt the greatest joy in the whole heaven and earth. A joy that doesn't diminish, but grows like a magic bean stalk, reaching the skies and beyond.

What's wrong?

Two weeks after I gave birth, my partner told his mother that I was just fine. It was the first time I wanted to strangle him. I am no whiner. But when would he register the fact that my hands were constantly frozen (some said "the aftermath of the anesthesia"), the cut across my tummy was still open, and my body was under the spell of gravity – ten thousand folds?

I didn't whine. But I did communicate my pain. And how could the one person, who should be sharing my joy and pain, be oblivious to the very excruciating conditions I was facing? Did joy blind him, or did it make him insensitive to my state? Was the baby all my spouse could think about? Sleep deprivation? Don't even try. It's nothing compared to what I went through.

I gave my husband credit for not having gone through the nine months of gestation, not carrying around across his tummy an ever-growing person, not having to deal with the hormonal fluctuation, not bothering with morning sickness, not suffering from weight gain and baby fat discomfort, not restraining from all kinds of food while ridiculously craving for them, not enduring acid reflux, not waking every hour in the depth of the night to release waste fluid for so-long-I- can't-even-say-it, and not having to do so-many-things-I-can't-even-list-them.

But as much as I was sympathetic toward him, I was just as angry that he, my spouse, was so out of touch with my body and its conditions. Was I taken for granted? I was no birth machine. I am a mother. A first-time mother. I was cut!

I felt so heavy. Physically. I couldn't open my eyes. How long had it been since the C-section? I don't give a frit about post-partum depression. What do I have to complain about?

I felt so heavy. Emotionally. I felt disconnected with the whole world. I didn't want to entertain the thought of me, having post-partum depression. I didn't plan on post-partum depression, and it shouldn't plan on me.

But I also knew that it was a very real possibility. Denial denied.

The Eve

Of all times, my husband chose to give me his cold the night I went to the hospital for a non-stress test. He was coughing with a running nose for a whole week before that. I kept asking him to go see a doctor. I was pregnant. I did not want to be stressed out about him getting sick, and my ultimate fear, him getting me sick.

My fear came true.

The non-stress test's results indicated that I needed an immediate C-section. We were admitted. I had nothing with me, except a head of hair crying out for a wash, and a developing fever. I started to have a migraine, a sore throat, and plenty of spite for my husband. This was the worst nightmare imaginable: I wanted a natural birth, full-term, with no medical intervention. "I won't be delivering. I will be delivered." I had lost control over my birth. It will now be in the hands of the OB and support staff.

The scheduled nurse was nice and courteous, but she wore such a strong perfume that every time she came in, I was coughing with teary eyes, my migraine worsened, my stomach turned and churned. Eventually, for my sake, she asked another nurse to care for me. But I was not receiving the care I needed. I was told to wait, and wait, and wait, even for a small request like a cup of water. My lovely husband was disoriented. He cried when he called home across the Atlantic, informing his parents of the early delivery. He was worried. Maybe scared.

I had no interest in crying.

My migraine was killing me. I had to ask the nurse five times before she remembered to give me the Tylenol. Just wonderful! Phlegm started to collect in my throat, and the urge to cough so often exacerbated my migraine. I just couldn't hate my husband enough.

I dozed off into the night, thinking it was a nightmare. I glanced over. My husband slept like an exhausted baby. I wasn't sure if I hated or loved him at that moment.

The Birth

My birth plan went out the window with the C-section. I spent a lot of time preparing, referencing, and finalizing the items on the plan. I even asked the OB to give my husband extra time with the umbilical cord, as he would be emotional and need his time.

I was rolled in early in the morning. Wired. IVed. Numbed.

I stayed calm, and did not fight the fact that my baby had to come out five weeks early. I did not have another choice. I focused on the moment.

It was months later that the suppressed anger of that moment burst out, spitting vomit everywhere. It came with all the hormonal shifts and fluid changes. What timing!

The only thing worth mentioning was, when the baby came out, I was under anesthesia, and could hear him cry. Loudly. Then he was brought to me, with my husband next to us. And I wouldn't see him until four hours later, even though I kept begging to see him.

The First Night

The commodious recovery room eased my claustrophobia. I had asked the nurse to place the baby on my arm, along my side, as soon as he was brought to me.

Even before the baby was born, my husband thought that he was the best father on earth. I admired his enthusiasm (I wouldn't call it ambition), but I rolled my eyes. He's barely a spoiled boy (yes, I'm guilty) and through the birth, I delivered him into manhood by making him a father; he kept sneaking back into his boy-land. How?

He was just his old self, a carefree and happy sleeper. I would clearly hear every single sound the baby made, but even when the alarm rang for the three hourly feedings, my husband was rock deaf. He was indeed a happy camper. And that's why I adored him to begin with. But it's quite impossible to adore him on my first post-partum night, calling out to him for 15 minutes in no vain for the feeding of our premie newborn.

The one image that stirred me, both with sympathy and anger – and maybe even love, was the image of my husband, his head dozed off in one direction, the baby's head moving in another direction, and the bottle sliding off his hand in yet another direction. A multi-directional collective. Hard proof of him as best father on earth. I took pity on him.

As the baby was strong and well, thanks to the buckets of water I drank every day and my super-healthy diet during pregnancy, we were discharged the next day. I was so happy to be going home.

No Milk! Won't latch!

The disasters didn't stop. I was pumping day and night, feeling deterred, dejected, depressed. And still, for two weeks, no milk.

I had no milk, as a result of my desiccated body and my five-week preterm delivery. I kept pumping to no avail. The baby refused to latch. I don't blame him. What is there to suck!

I called the whole world. My sisters. La Leche League. My lactationist at the hospital. Local lactation consultants. No one could help.

The baby continued to refuse to latch, even long after I produced ample milk. He didn't latch for the first two months. In a moment of hopelessness, I concluded that he was stubborn, just like his father.

I was skin-and-bone, like a stick. My pre-pregnancy cloths were loose on me. I was wiped out in every sense of the word. I had no appetite. I knew I had to eat to make milk, so I ate. But lactation was still a foreign idea to my body. My breasts challenged my patience and hope. I couldn't cry. I was so exhausted, overwhelmed, dead. I couldn't sleep at night. I felt nothing but pain and numbness. And frustration. Burning frustration.

I kept padding my breasts with hot towels, too hot that my husband screamed when he had to help fetch them for me. But I counted on these towels to pull the milk out. So I endured the burning heat. Still nothing.

I started eating like mad. In two weeks, I gained 30 pounds. It was the most uncomfortable thing I went through in my entire life. I ate everything that people said 'milk-producing.' I didn't want to miss a chance. Still, two weeks, 30 pounds more, and no milk.

I researched all the water bodies in the world. The longest rivers. The largest oceans. I recited their names, writing poems about them, calling on them, thinking of streams of water pouring into my body flow.

After these tireless efforts, I felt an overpowering sense of despair.

I felt guilt: that my baby was premature, that he did not have a natural birth, that he had to go on formula because I did not lactate. I felt pain: the pain that I was robbed of a vaginal birth that I preferred and prepared for, the pain that came from the incision, the pain that came with all the fluids shifting in my desiccated body.

I lacerated my husband's pride with unreserved candor. I had no patience left for him. I was too worried about the baby's sake, I just couldn't tolerate any nonsense. One night, my husband took a half an hour to wake up for the baby's 3 am feeding. And as he was dozing off with the baby and bottle in his arms, I gritted my teeth: "If you can't wake up at 3 am to feed your infant, then don't release your sperms."

That didn't do much for my husband at the moment. But somehow, the admonition resurfaced the next day (take a good guess why). And he laughed, in fact, he couldn't stop laughing for a long time. He said that he admired the fact that though I was in so much pain and discomfort, I didn't lose my sense of humor. Except that the humor was not intended. I was dead serious.

The Loss

Motherhood brought as many things as it took away. I could no longer sleep in peace. I either attended to the baby, lingered over his sight and kept kissing him for the ten thousandth time, or washed bottles. Or did laundry. Or cleaned up.

I know that I no longer have control over my heart. The baby does.

I know that my head doesn't always lead the decision, and I force myself to make all the efforts in the world to stay focused and decisive.

Holding my baby in my arms, I knew that I had lost the sense of compromise. I would not yield to anything for his sake and his safety. My fingers were so dry, they cracked like caked mud. I did not care. If I must wash bottles and flanges thrice a day, so I will. If I need to ask guests to wash their hands before touching my baby, I won't be shy about it (or I'd have no guests). If I need to bring the moon down for my baby to play with, I probably would've.

I lost my sense of relativity. I know my priority. I know what is important. I know what is real. I became wise in spite of my physical setbacks. I was not afraid to tell my husband about my honest thoughts, be them crude and raw. I lost my sense of modesty. I will tell you that I am the most wonderful mother on earth, and that no one has ever loved anyone else as much as I love my child. I even made up a song, in the rap style, to sing of my boundless love. And I sang it to my baby day and night. It goes like this, "I love you most on earth, I love you more than anyone can love you, I love you more than the whole world can love you." Quite a bold claim, but I am sure it is accurate.

I lost my sense of privacy. The child owned it. And it was quite an amazing feeling to totally let go. Like when you make love. Or when you dream. I no longer get angry at my husband. I lost my anger. I remember what a kind and loving person he has always been. And I forgave him (yes, I'm the ruler, and am never at fault!) for having caused me anger. Going through the birth, he might have suffered second-hand pain and all of that. But maybe that's how it should be. He shared in my pain, so that he can bathe in my joy. We have the same foibles: we would hover over our sleeping baby, taking in each of his breath, acting like clumsy dorks waiting for the shooting stars.

I've lost myself. Sixteen months after the birth, I realized that the little rascal came from me, but he doesn't belong to me. Quite the contrary.

Joy Interrupted

Mother with Cancer
by Alan Nolan

When we arrived
there was shit in
the passage
the kitchen lino
bedroom carpet
a mop and bottle of bleach
stood by the toilet door

you thought
it would bother you
cleaning it up
but it was like
looking after
a baby
your baby.

On Being Lucky, and Not
by Kim Hensley Owens

I was one of the lucky ones.

Married at the tail end of 30 and immediately "trying," I was a mother at 31. No waiting month after month, after month, after month, for a plus sign that never appeared. No loss at seven weeks. No crippling loneliness with news no one knows. No pregnancy inexplicably turned malignancy. No loss at 10 weeks, or 11. No holding back tears or fumbling for words at the hundredth well-meaning "When are you guys going to get down to business and have a kid?" No D & C. No blighted ovum bathing a pregnancy test in HCG, masquerading as a pregnancy later described instead as an "empty gestational sac." No cramping, bleeding, and crying at 12 weeks, or 16, or 20. No certificate of loss inexplicably bearing tiny cheerful-seeming baby footprints in pastel colors. No wrenching news and heartbreaking decision at four months. No lying. No crib assembled but never used. No stilled heartbeat at 26 or 28 weeks. No daylong induced hospital labor with the sad outcome already known. No naming ceremony for a baby who never took a breath.

I was one of the lucky ones.

But many of my friends—that's them up there, not named, but loved—weren't. Some have since become mothers. Some later experienced complication-free pregnancies. Some adopted. Some made it through months of bed rest, or tens of thousands of dollars worth of fertility treatments. Some drank herbal Chinese teas and got pregnant. Some drank herbal Chinese teas and didn't. Some gave up.

I was one of the lucky ones.

One child two years old, I tried for another. And got one. No surprise "secondary infertility." No carefully timed second pregnancy lost at 9 weeks, or 11. No waiting to try again. No wondering what went wrong. No absent heartbeat at 20 weeks, when everything had seemed fine. No crappy labor for a baby who isn't. No clinging to tiny living children who don't understand what's wrong. No explaining that there won't be a new sibling after all. No sobbing on the due date, a day etched with lost hope. No trying again. No losing again.

I was one of the lucky ones.

But many of my friends—yes, that's them, too, up there, not named, but loved—weren't.

I was one of the lucky ones.

A mother! A wonderful thing to be! And yet one woman I know, an older professor—old enough to be my mother—tells the story of her own pregnancy loss as an almost-joyous occasion. Before legalized abortion, before she went to graduate school, before she married, she fell pregnant (this is how the Brits describe it, and in this context it works particularly well), much to her dismay. But one night early on, as she was "leaping about onstage," her pregnancy fell from her—this loss welcome, she never did become a mother. She considers

77

herself one of the lucky ones, too, this loss read instead as a restoration, without her having, or having to make, a choice.

I was one of the lucky ones.

And what of those who do not so much lose a pregnancy, as choose to lose one? They, too, experience loss—deeply inarticulate losses tied as they are to political, social, religious, and moral morasses. I've never known a woman who openly mourned an aborted chance at motherhood. Nor have I known a woman who celebrated that kind of loss. Though precious few share anything at all about such losses.

Some women do choose loss. Two teenage friends got pregnant. One chose loss. One chose single teenage motherhood. Both felt loss. Neither felt lucky.

One woke up, hung over, naked, next to a man she vaguely remembered meeting the night before. She had overindulged in alcohol because she was staying the night at the hosts' home—wouldn't have to drive, would be perfectly safe, could drown her sorrows and hide her insecurities.

"You're so lucky," we said the next day, not yet knowing the full story, when she confessed she could not remember anything past 10 pm. Lucky she was with friends, "safe." Lucky that these good friends let her, blind drunk, enter and stay the night in a closed bedroom with a man she didn't know? Lucky these good friends had a shower in which she could crouch, sobbing, after she heard that man's answer to her bewildered "What happened?" Lucky her good friends—who did know—let her leave without suggesting she visit a pharmacy, a clinic, or a doctor on her way home? Lucky she got pregnant when she had no partner, no job, and was living with her mother?

But she was pregnant. Until she chose not to be. She mourned the lost chance. She worried she would never be a mother. But she forgave herself. And that loss, that chosen loss, enabled her, later, married, employed, living as an adult, to be one of the lucky ones.

Another friend found herself pregnant four months into her nine month engagement, with an elaborate, expensive, and family-fraught wedding planned, a dress already purchased. Crippled by expectations, even "in this day and age," she, too, though happily attached and employed, chose loss to save face. (She's not the first, not the last.) And she, too, was later a lucky one: motherhood lost, then found.

I was one of the lucky ones.

But some of my friends—yes, that's them up there, too, not named, but loved—weren't. Or weren't in the sense of lucky as "get married and then have a baby," but were lucky in other ways. Sometimes the loss itself is somehow lucky, but far more often, for the women I know, the loss is far from lucky, the recovery far from quick, whatever the circumstance.

These losses—these many, many losses, of all different kinds, are only the stories I know. There are more: losses upon losses.

Thirty percent of all pregnancies end in miscarriage or stillbirth. 30%. So it is not, should not be, surprising that I have two aunts who miscarried, a grandmother who miscarried twice, another who miscarried once, a stepsister and at least two teachers who miscarried, and friend after friend after friend after friend until the number of losses I know of reaches beyond what I can count with my fingers and my toes, far beyond even what my many teeth could help me tally. And those are only the ones I know about.

Most women don't tell. They don't get chocolate or flowers or condolence notes when they lose a pregnancy. They don't get special treatment at work when several weeks of secret, flushed anticipation, shifts abruptly to a hormonally disrupted private nightmare. Far too many feel loss alone. (Can partners understand? I suspect not, though surely many try.)

I was one of the lucky ones.

With no loss to share, but losses shared with me, I lend my voice to those who have lost, but do not speak. Who do not speak of unspoken assumptions, of traditional or problematic expectations, of inquiries that impose values and judgments. Of the burden that is the expectation to have, or not to have, a baby at various points in a woman's life.

Women are discouraged from speaking of early pregnancies for fear they'll be lost, but then experience loss alone if it comes. An unwitting societal conspiracy masks the normalcy of loss—and it is normal—and makes the experience of loss worse. Loss that is invisible, unshareable feels unthinkable, unendurable.

After the magical 12-week point where family and friends have been let into the fold, after neighbors and co-workers are aware of a pregnancy, women are encouraged to feel safe. But loss can still happen, is sometimes still chosen, for reasons complex. Such as when a test reveals a fetus who can't survive after birth: choices are made. Sometimes chosen losses, losses conducted in shame and pain, chosen losses often described as something else.

Losses chosen suffer the deepest taboo. Women may have legal freedom to choose, but they do not have societal freedom to tell.

I was one of the lucky ones.

Some of my friends weren't—that's them up there, not named, but loved—and I wrote this for them.

Plea

There comes an hour when begging stops,
When the long interceding lips
Perceive their prayer is vain.
"Thou shalt not" is a kinder sword
Than from a disappointing God
"Disciple, call again."

Emily Dickinson, "There comes an hour when begging stops"

"Baby Blue and the missing part" - Michèle AimPée Parent

We make deals all the time. We promise ourselves if we eat one piece of cake we will exercise the next day. We promise we will get a project at work done as long as we are compensated. But, what happens when we have nothing to give in return or we have no hopes of ever getting what we want? We beg and we plead. We hope for some sort of mercy, some sort of relief.

Sometimes our pleading comes in the form of wishes, such as in Valerie Murrenus Pilmaier's "Impotent wishes." I have spent years on wishes that would never come true. These wishes often have a certain unreality to them, almost as is if you are in a dream hoping to never wake up. I felt this unreality in Olivia Good's "The Island," in which the cutting pain of now is tempered by the moments of escape.

Our mind protects us in many ways, sometimes in the form of rationalizations and wondering why. Like Samantha, in "A Lost and Found Me: A Mother's Work in Progress," I have spent time trying to understand the context of my losses. The context helps us make sense of our loss, but so many times our questions go unanswered, as in Janeen McGuire's "20 Questions for My Daughter's Birth Mother."

I see bargaining as a way to cope with the "No" a trauma gives us. We tell the pain to stop and if it does, we will do anything in return. We say we will do anything to have prevented a loss. It is a constant state of "If only if." I see the ifs in Liz Dolan's "Deliver Us." I visualize a small plea echoing through the chambers of denial. So often these pleas are unanswered when we are in the darkest wake of our loss.

While reading the pieces I selected for this section, I often wanted to make this plea or I would grieve as the writers and/or their characters begged for mercy. I could not answer their pleas, such as those I felt in Merrill Edlund's "When I miss my kids" and Jenn Williamson's "March for Love." I couldn't even answer my own. But, in the act of listening, of hearing those pleas, I felt a little less alone. I felt less alone when I read Trangđài Glassey-Trầnguyễn's "what would I do after a miscarriage?" and Svetlana Bochman's "The Favorite Child, or, Pregnancy After Loss." I wasn't the only one disappointed, wanting what had been to not be.

This section could be the most relatable. I haven't met anyone grieving a loss who didn't wish the loss to not have occurred. Our minds bounce back between what might have been and what is, like I saw in Ivan Jim Saguibal Layugan's "True Story." We are often stuck in the nostalgia of our loss, driven by the pleas that can't be answered. And the sister to nostalgia, metaphor, is another way of coping, as we can see in Lori Lamothe's "Skating with Tropes."

The only way these pleas ever be answered is to ask for something different, asking for something that can be. Please let me get through the day. Please let me hurt a little less. We don't see these pleas as a bargain, offering something in return. We stop making deals. We surrender to what is and what will be. I see this surrender in Jenn Williamson's "Driving Back to Ridgeway from Telluride, CO, mid-August."

At least this is what I felt as I read the pieces in this section.

Pleas made way for peace.

Joy, Interrupted

Impotent wishes
by Valerie Murrenus Pilmaier

When I allow myself to wish for the impossible, which is a rare as I no longer believed in the possibility of the impossible, I obviously first wish that my daughter Chavalah was still alive; but more to the point, I wish that I had stayed home with her that frigid December day, like I had wanted to, and spent the day playing with her rather than receiving, one hour and twenty two minutes after I dropped her off at daycare, the breathless and frantic call from my husband that stated, "There is something wrong with the baby."

I wish that I hadn't arrived to a daycare ablaze with lights from the police chief's vehicle, the fire truck and the ambulance. I wish I didn't have to hear the woman I entrusted my precious child to for three hours, two times a week, say to me, "She stopped breathing. I put her on her tummy in the crib and walked away to take care of another child – it couldn't have been more than a minute" – words that somehow did not show up in the police report. I wish I didn't have to feel the helplessness within myself and from the EMT when he said, "We're trying so hard; we can't get her to breathe. We're taking her to St. Mike's but you can't ride in the ambulance."

I wish I didn't have to walk through the emergency doors to see my ten week old baby, wearing only a diaper on a day with a negative wind-chill, strapped down to a table filled with pumps and tubes, while hordes of people surrounded her. I wish I didn't know what it is like to look at my husband and realize that the person we both loved most, the one we had wished for, was dying.

I wish I didn't know what it was to wish so hard, to want my daughter to come back so fervently, that I believe I willed her spirit to obey me so that her heart started beating after having had no life function for too long. I wish I didn't know the useless hope and optimism I felt after the heartbeat came back, so much so that when the doctors decided to rush her to Children's Hospital after she stabilized and asked us to accompany her in the ambulance, I sat chatting in the ambulance with the EMTS on the way there while they reassured me, "Children are resilient. Children are resilient," as I held my baby's hand and couldn't understand why her body was so very cold.

I wish I hadn't believed in miracles, so that when the emergency doctor said, "You know, there is nothing we can do. She didn't have a heartbeat for fifty-three minutes (fifty-three minutes! – a fact no one until then had bothered to tell us). She is going to die." I wish I hadn't just been hit with the realization that there was no magical intervention that would occur, causing me to lose all muscle control and crumple into a ball on the floor.

I wish I had spent every last second holding my daughter, instead of going to the waiting rooms and calling friends and family to come because I could not face the finality and brutality on my own. I wish I hadn't been so calm when the attending doctor came to tell us that all of Chava's organs were failing and we needed to make a decision.

I wish I had been able to scream the way my husband did when we watched her heartbeat slowly stop after turning the machines off. I wish I hadn't heard my husband's heart breaking as he held our now lifeless child, while I sat next to him in complete shock, my own heart broken and my body not yet comprehending that I no longer had an infant to feed, my breasts so hard and painful from milk that would never be suckled.

I wish I didn't know what it was like to have the conversation with the Organ Donation lady about what parts they could have and which ones "wouldn't be of any use." I wish I didn't have to leave that conversation to find my silent daughter, all alone on a table, washed and wrapped in a new blanket and think how could we have left her, even for one minute, by herself?

I wish I didn't have to make funeral arrangements with an asshole named Vic who excitedly told us that she could be buried in a section known as "Babyland" and who tried to sell us a family plot so that he could make extra commission right before Christmas.

I wish I hadn't had to go home to our now too silent house to pick up things so that we could stay at my husband's parents' house because the sight and touch of anything belonging to my child made my very viscera ache.

I wish I didn't know what it was like to be summoned to the phone from a dream of the first moment I met my daughter, naked and screaming on my chest, to answer incessant questions from the Organ Donation place and screaming through hysterical sobs, "Yes, I agree to the organ donation."

I wish I didn't know what it was like to burst into tears at any given moment because my body would only let me momentarily acknowledge the enormity of what I had just lost.

I wish I didn't know what it was like to hear a coroner sobbing on the phone and saying, "She was so beautiful and perfect. We couldn't' find any reason for her death. No reason at all."

I wish I didn't have to shop for funeral clothes in the midst of Christmas shopping season and be asked by a salesgirl to sing a Christmas carol to get a discount on my black funeral dress and black funeral clothes, thus forcing me to say out loud for the first time, "My baby just died." I wish I hadn't seen the look of irritation on the salesgirl's face because I had just ruined her day.

I wish I didn't know what it was like to select a coffin, walk behind my friends and brothers carrying it, watch it be lowered into the ground and then personally throw dirt on it to bury my baby.

I wish I didn't know how painful it is to rejoin a world that didn't know or care that we had just lost the most important thing in our lives.

I wish I didn't know what it was like to walk into my daughter's room and lay on the ground for hours just so that I could smell her scent and be around the things she touched.

I wish I didn't know what it was like to look into my husband's eyes and see the depths of sadness that mirrored my own, to be numb to everything, and feel guilty when I wasn't crying and helpless when I was.

I wish I didn't know what it was like to suddenly become the "one with the dead baby" and see people consciously avoiding me when I approached because they did not know how to talk to me, or, worse, to hear "It must be God's Plan" and "She is in a better place now" from all the well-meaning but clueless people who never lost a child and had no idea what absolute bullshit they were spewing.

I wish I didn't know what it was like to start sobbing in the card aisle while reading Mother's Day cards because I knew that I would never receive this type of card from her, nor would I ever be able to give her one for becoming a mother.

I wish I didn't know what it was like to hear people say, "So are you trying to replace Chava?" when they found out that I was pregnant with my second child, also a girl.

I wish I didn't pray for the dreams between asleep and awake where I can still smell her, feel her, and hear her voice because waking from those dreams devastated me.

I wish I didn't wake up screaming at least once a month, still, after six years, because the traumatic wound is still fresh in my head.

Joy, Interrupted

I wish that I still knew how to believe in the God of my childhood – the one who could make miracles happen if I prayed hard enough. I wish I could believe in any God, really, because then I could also believe in a Heaven where I could spend eternity with my baby.

I wish that my take-home message from this experience had been something other than that there is absolutely nothing positive that can ever be gleaned from the death of my child.

But most of all, I wish that I knew for certain that absolutely nothing could have been done to prevent it because the uncertainty haunts me every day of my life.

Driving Back to Ridgeway from Telluride, CO, mid-August
by Jenn Williamson

We were running late, delayed
by the end-of-summer rain that had threatened
all afternoon to break, finally,

because we couldn't waste the sunlight
and hiked the old, gravel mining trail, for the view
of trees darkening like moss

and no sign of the town below, hidden
somewhere in the leaves and looming gray rock,
so that the light grew weaker

until the rain was tipping over
and pulling us down the mountain, and it was
suddenly evening and then night.

The rain stopped, and we had three hours
of road ahead. I promised to sit up with you,
your husband asleep behind us.

I'm sure we talked in the blue-lit darkness,
but I don't remember the words, just the sense
that you were really in the car with me,

that you didn't need to say anything
about Mom's cancer because everything we said
was about her cancer and about the lives

we were slowly making in each
bewildering flash of uncertain movement.
In an instant, we both saw them—

two greenish-yellow eyes, and then
the lean body of a doe next to the road, head raised,
determining whether to turn back

or stand her ground. We passed her slowly
and continued our climb out of another black valley,
road layering back and forth

like discarded ribbon. In the dark,
you don't see the descent, you just start to feel it.
The car noses downward,

the whole body shifts slightly in response,
so that you're not straining your head forward
but pushing it back.

Descending the tiers, each turn brought more deer—
another three, another five or seven, grazing, licking the rain
from grass on the slope or shoulders.

At the car's approach, they watched us as silently
as we watched them. We must have seen forty, maybe fifty,
before regaining the next valley.

The darkness on either side flattened with the road,
but you were stiff, fearful of a sudden dash across.
We were on the mesa when it happened:

you saw them just in time and stopped. Two elk,
bark-brown and just hinting winter's mossy coat around
the neck and shoulders, towered onto the road.

They stopped and looked back at us,
eyes reflecting the headlights, glowing—not with fear
or even uncertainty. Maybe it was resignation.

A smaller elk hobbled out of the brush.
Adolescent, it moved as though its back legs
were slightly longer than its front. I couldn't tell

if it made noises, but I imagined it
lowing, pitiful, calling to the others. It turned as if
to look at us, but the largest nudged it

on the side, urged it to the edge of the road,
where they drifted back, turning into the brush,
didn't glance at us again.

The Island
by Olivia Good

Disoriented and groggy, I tried to determine my location. Where was I? How did I get here? The cruel, glaring light of the sun beating down on my upturned face was the first sensation that greeted me as I opened my eyes on the desolate beach. I turned my head away, as if that act would allow me to slip back into the darkness of the night before. What day was it? Still Tuesday? I reached down instinctively for my swollen belly, only to be crushed by the surge of reality that had eluded me upon waking. Where, for months, a small, round bulge had grown, now, was only a fleshy emptiness that penetrated deep into my soul. Rolling over in despair, I sobbed into the ground that would soon swallow up my precious baby, not caring that the sand was filling my mouth, nose, and eyes.

I was no more certain of how long I sat there crying than I was of how I had arrived on that lonely beach. Before my arrival, my last memory was of the hospital: The cold steel of the bed, the low hum of the medical equipment, my utter aloneness in the darkness. The world, which my beautiful child would never open her eyes to see, had likewise refused to cast even a glance upon her. Amidst a haze of pain-numbing drugs and sedatives, I barely felt my body writhe with contractions as I slept. When the once much-anticipated moment of delivery finally arrived, I lacked the strength and the will to call for assistance in the pitch-black room as I strained to free my daughter from the prison that had so tragically failed her, listening to the driving rain beat down upon the windows behind me. The delivery was easy. Such a small baby, there was little pushing to be done. At last, with nothing more for me to do, the nurse was paged. She placed that tiny piece of me in a plastic tray, inspected her for signs of imperfection or the likely cause of her demise, and then set her on the counter to await the doctor's assessment as I looked on, helplessly.

I wondered how much time had passed since that night. Had I given birth just hours before, or had it been days, months, or even years? Had my body succumbed to my heart's desire to perish with my child and did I find myself now in some kind of afterlife so radically different from the one I had anticipated? It didn't matter.

I stared out at the sea, feeling the foam of the waves against my toes. I backed up, onto the dry sand, picking up a rough stone from the beach, replaying the scene in the hospital room following my daughter's birth. "I saw Dan in the waiting room," my mother was saying. "He said that all you do is cry and cry. You're not the only one affected by this. You have to think of his feelings too. You're not helping him by crying all the time," she scolded solemnly. The nurse was standing at the foot of my bed, once again holding the plastic tray containing my daughter's lifeless body, her eyes sad and sympathetic, but lacking the words to match. "I know you're not ready to hear this yet, but these things happen all the time. You can't dwell on it. Perhaps with medication…" Her voice trailed off, as she critiqued my mental state. "You know," she continued, "I had a friend to whom the very same thing happened. She turned around and had a baby the next year, just like nothing happened. You've just got to move on."

I rolled their words over and over in my mind, each time allowing them to scorch me, like the sun on my back. With the incoming tide, scores of tiny smooth sea stones washed up on the beach, and as I looked at them, I noticed a bottle swaying in the current. I ventured out into the water to retrieve it. I was shocked by how pristine it was. After prying the cork from the neck of the bottle, I discovered a note written on a ragged piece of paper.

"I'm so sorry for your loss. You know, perhaps it is better this way. Things like this seem to just be nature's way of taking care of children who would have insurmountable disabilities. I'm sure you'll have another soon."

Joy, Interrupted

I stared at the paper, first in disbelief, then in shock, then in anger, before throwing it with all of my might, back into the sea from which it came. I fell back upon the sand in outrage. How could people—trained professionals, like the nurse; loving family members, like my mother; strangers, like the author of this note—be so insensitive? From where had that note come and who had sent it? I began to wonder exactly how far I was from other pieces of land, and from my questioning emerged a cold fear unlike any I had previously experienced.

Where was I, and would I ever find my way back to the place I had been before? Vaguely I remembered that other place, where I had happily spent my summer nurturing flowers and vegetables, and my autumn anticipating the arrival of my new baby. There was happiness there, and shade. Here, there was no escape from the sun's glaring rays. The hospital was somewhere else, too. Certainly it was not in that other place that still existed on the fringes of my memory, but also, it was not here. I also wondered where my baby was, and wondered if she understood far more about the nature of grief, time, and love than I now did.

As I pondered the anomaly in the space-time continuum in which I now seemed to find myself, I decided to take a walk around the perimeter of the island to clear my head. As I meandered across the sand, I came across another note-filled bottle. Though not as polished as the previous bottle, its stationary was crisp and clean.

"I'm so sorry to hear about what happened to your baby. Though I don't know what you're feeling, know that I am feeling for you in this difficult time."

I nodded instinctively, as if the kind-hearted person who had written those words were standing before me. I placed the bottle and its contents on the sand and continued with my walk.

Before long, I noticed another bottle bobbing in the surf in front of me. The current seemed to drive this bottle directly toward me, and it washed up at my feet. The bottle looked as if it had been tossed and turned by the ocean for quite some time. The paper on which the note inside was written was neat, but faded, though the words were still clearly legible.

"I've been trying to call you in this difficult time, but since you don't seem to want companionship right now, I decided to write a little note. I once was where you are. I know it is a lonely place, but know that you are only permanently banished to its shores if you choose to be. Let the ocean carry you back. I know it is difficult to trust it, but it is the only way to return. It may take months, years, or even a lifetime, but you will find your way back, if you allow the current to carry you. If you need anything, just call."

I stared at the parchment through tear-filled eyes, and glanced out at the sea. Only then did I realize that in all of my misery here on the island, I had not once heard the sound of the ocean, until that very moment. It seemed to beckon me, and I had no desire to ignore its call. I walked out into the waves, not to sink into oblivion, as I might have considered an hour earlier, but to float into the salty water, which would both sting and heal my wounds, relishing the sensation of its coolness against my sunburned skin.

As I allowed the swirling, endless blue to surround me, I thought of all of the countless other bottles nearby. How many would have angered me, as the first one had? I didn't know, and it didn't matter. The ocean was carrying them far from me. Floating, eyes turned upward, bathed in the soothing waters, I could feel the waves carrying me at will, and I knew that someday, that same merciful current that diverted painful unknown messages away from me would return a transformed, salt-worn version of myself to that land from which I came.

The Favorite Child, or, Pregnancy After Loss
by Svetlana Bochman

Dearest child,
Every ultrasound image
Helps to see you more clearly
Soon, with God's help
I will see you face to face

Your sister died
One month before her birth
And as different as you will be from her -
(You will live, you will grow)
Have a different appearance, a separate personality,
So am I unlike my self
Of six months ago (when she died)
Of one year ago
When she lived within me

In this new pregnancy journal
I write of my hopes for you
Rather than my hopes for me
I treasure these fuzzy images of you
Rather than putting them aside
I listen for the life inside
For I cannot assume it is there

When I saw her sonogram
I smiled and called her Tadpole
When I saw your face
I cried tears of joy and called you Angel

In preparing for her
I thought of the material.
Now the clothes, toys and bassinet are put away;
In preparing for you
I think of the spiritual
And pray every day for your safe delivery
(For a successful birth is neither a material nor an intellectual
        endeavor.
It is a miraculous one)

Joy, Interrupted

Deliver Us
by Liz Dolan

When mother was wee
the midwife Big Mary
trudged down the lonen
bundled in a black cape
billowed by winds off the Irish Sea
whistling through black night
over the roof of the flax mill
and through the red barn's shingles.

On their table, flat bread, fresh butter
and red berries in clotted cream glowed
while over kindling crackling
in the Kilcoo hearth, water roiled blue.

Her cheeks persimmon, barely able to
kneel still, mother
prayed with her father
befuddled when he squeezed her
thin fingers till blackthorn beads
chafed. From her mother's groans
in the room below the larder
she kenned she would soon snuggle the nursling
she thought Big Mary had ferried

under her cape. Years later,
across the waters
far from the mountain rill
spilling past her cottage,
cape-less doctors and starched nurses
with radiant tools
delivered three of mother's bairn
dead, shrouded by a white room
in a cast iron, barred-bed.
A silver-embossed radiator hissed
beneath a brick-walled window.

Sweet Little One
by Lottie Corley

For the child I can never bare,
I rub my tummy though there's nothing there.
No baby to kick inside of me,
Or to ponder what they'll grow up to be.
I can't teach them how to ride a bike,
Or get those sweet little kisses good night.
No, I won't get to see my children play,
Was there something I did and now I must pay?
Feeling this miracle is not in my favor,
Nor the awesome experience of going through labor.
No Santa, no Easter or the tooth fairy,
No rushing to my arms because the movie was scary.
No precious mementos from their young little life,
I guess I'll just end up a motherless wife.
I've waited too long, that's what I fear,
I feel the sorrow of giving up near.
No hearing "I do" or their baby cry,
All this I'll miss dear lord tell me why.
No diaper to change, no boo boo to kiss.
No penny in the fountain for them to wish.
Dear God where's my sweet little one?
I long for a daughter I long for a son.

Joy, Interrupted

A Lost and Found Me: A Mother's Work In Progress
by Samantha

"I had lost nearly thirty-seven years to the image I carried of myself. I had ambushed myself by believing, to the letter, my parents' definition of me. My parents had succeeded in making me a stranger to myself. They had turned me into an exact image of what they needed at the time, and because there was something essentially complaisant and orthodox in my nature, I allowed them to knead and shape me into the smooth lineaments of their nonpareil child. ... I longed for their approval, their applause, their pure uncomplicated love for me, and I looked for it years after I realized they were not even capable of letting me have it. To love one's children is to love oneself, and this was a state of supererogatory grace denied my parents by birth and circumstance. I needed to reconnect to something I had lost. Somewhere I had lost touch with the kind of man I had the potential of being. I needed to effect reconciliation with that unborn man and try to coax him gently towards his maturity."

Tom in The Price of Tides, by Pat Conroy

Becoming a mother

Anger's flames ringed my childhood; I learned to tread carefully, too carefully, perhaps. Mine was a life lived for my parents' anger – to abate it, quell it, manage it; even at times to feed it. My life belonged to them.

When I had my first child at 34 in Costa Rica, just having left my 20th or so job, the tailspin from the stress of birth and my son's early childhood was an unexpected and difficult first step on a path to understand and unite my splintered self.

Becoming a mother meant I had to make hard decisions and take losses to reclaim my life, without which I wouldn't be able to be present, nor be a spontaneous, playful and flexible mother.

A wakeful infant, avid nurser, and an early walker, my son required an extremely attentive caregiver who could quickly understand his needs. I had few calm moments in which to take care of my basic needs, never mind ponder the reality of my new life as a mother.

The new and constant demands of being a mother, combined with broken sleep, triggered deep issues from my childhood.

In a deep, amorphous way, I started to sense a familiarity in all this stress and confusion of my son's early years. I realized at a certain point that I had done a similar disappearing act before; but when I was a child it hadn't been for a good cause, nor had there been much redemption to the act. As a child and well into adulthood, my customary posture, albeit largely unconscious, was to twist and submerge my own needs and desires to attune myself to others' needs and expectations.

These skills that I had cultivated as a child were actually quite essential during my son's infancy. They allowed me to anticipate his movements and meet his unspoken needs. As he grew, though, and I had a daughter, these ingrained behaviors were starting to get in the way of being a good mother.

Trying to please others doesn't mix well with championing your kids' needs, standing up for them, getting them what they need, never mind taking care of yourself, which is critical in balancing the constant demands of parenting.

This "disassociation" from my deepest self is something I've had to learn to slough off. When I became a parent I had to stop playing defense and get on offense to engage with the ways abuse and neglect had cocooned my feelings, creativity and intuition.

A good mother is her own person

Over time I saw that my kids wanted me first and foremost to be present and available. They wanted me to be myself, however imperfect, unpolished or hesitant that self was. This was a wondrous, albeit sometimes painful realization, as I wasn't used to being valued on my own terms. Of course, it wouldn't hurt if I also had good instincts, a lot of common sense, a bunch of bravery, and also a calm head to chart unpredictable, sometimes challenging or even scary situations.

This was daunting, as I was a novice at trusting and knowing myself. Yet it was also freeing. Could I overcome my fears of inadequacy to do this for them? I had to try. This could be one of life's greatest opportunities to practice these truncated skills. By giving my kids what they needed, it seemed I would simultaneously be giving myself the tools and skills I needed to create other healthy relationships and patterns in my life.

As I dusted off a more genuine self and had access to parts of myself previously hidden, I realized I had very little tolerance for unhealthy or one-sided relationships. I also became allergic to demands that seemed excessively draining, or requests that didn't respect my talents, unique perspective or my new limitations as a mother.

This led to me start saying "No" to all kinds of things. This previously unused muscle was hard to train and tone! Whereas the previous me would have signed up to run a committee, to make things happen, to carry more than my share of weight in different circumstances, I now saw and felt very clearly how unfulfilling most of these activities and some relationships were. My simple lack of time and energy, especially after my second child was born in 2008, meant that if I didn't ration myself, I'd have very little to give to my kids.

My initial disappearing act, when my kids were young, in which I submerged my own needs to meet their urgent and multiple needs, allowed for this new family of my own to evolve.

As I came to understand that this new set of relations was very much under my control, unlike my family of origin over which I had little control as a child and teen, I saw there was room for me to have my own voice and presence. In fact, my new family could actually stand in contrast to my childhood, and be a place where I was required to stop hiding and to be present as my genuine self.

Adult survivor of childhood neglect and abuse

I can live in the service of resentment, regret, anger and hate, or I can live for that part of myself that wasn't allowed a voice or given room to be herself. The latter is the only way as a mother I have any hope of breaking the cycle of abuse and neglect I experienced.

Joy, Interrupted

As a child, feeling would have meant I existed separately from my parents, and this would have been very threatening to them due to what I now can see was a social or mental disorder.

Rather than have desires and needs that derived from my own feelings, I sought safety in disappearing. This created a sort of splintered off self that hid when the going got rough, and took cover from physical abuse, criticism, judgment, and lack of nurturing.

I became a quiet, over-achieving, "good girl" while growing up. I cushioned my life in the innocent ways children do: talking only to select adults, sucking my thumb for a decade, and immersing myself in my own interests. I figured most people weren't telling me the truth, since my parents didn't. "Love" meant they resented my existence, and that didn't ring very true to me.

Over time, these coping mechanisms translated into a position of defeat – I wouldn't challenge directly, I would shrink, or find a way around things; I wouldn't hope for myself, only attune myself to others' needs. Defeat's counterpart, defiance, naturally reared its gnarly head from time to time. I was good at hiding – under my bed, up in trees, lost in my own thoughts, quiet. These protective adaptations, while they made me good at reading other people's emotions, blocked me from having a proactive approach to my life.

My schooling and jobs were first and foremost about living up to what I imagined were others' expectations. The deep, underlying agenda of my public undertakings was to try to impress my father, and to prove to my mother that I was independent and didn't need her. My letters and phone calls to them were about my salary, or important sounding titles, because I knew that was what they wanted to hear. It wasn't what I cared about or needed to talk about.

Yet, conversely, whenever I did succeed, it was a blow to my mother, who was disappointed with her own life. So, in retrospect, I see that if I did aim high, I managed to find a way to do just so-so enough to make both my father have something to brag about, and yet not make my mother seethe with jealousy.

As children, my younger sister and I learned to stay alert for signs my father would blow so we could scurry upstairs before he could hit us with whatever he could grab – we won maybe half the time. This escaping, as dramatic as it sounds, was in fact much easier than avoiding and managing the unspoken expectations, the silent, omnipresent needs of my parents that seemed to weight our every move, thought and feeling.

These firewalls I erected, as effective as they were as a child, over time served the unintended purpose of making parts of myself inaccessible. It became easier to be superficial in my dealings with others, to not let my intuition reign in important decisions and situations, and to hunker down into various forms of isolation. All this allowed anger to smolder deep down. I buried my true self deeply, and let it out in ways that felt safe: with a few loving extended family members, with pets, in nature and through books. Later music, sports, and Eastern philosophies and practices, as well as honest and caring friendships, allowed me to access my inner world in new ways and gave me footholds to climb up into a new reality.

My life thankfully also included wonderfully supportive and loving relatives, so I did learn other modes of being and behaving. But as a child growing up in a 1970s modern nuclear family, the stress in my home had an inordinate impact on me.

Shaking off maladaptive behaviors

By many traditional yardsticks I had "nothing to complain about." I didn't lack for nutritious food, clothing, medical care, schooling, or recreation. The outward signs of a middle class household meant that we were not a family typically considered abusive. These stereotypes meant our neglect and abuse went undetected, unreported and unaddressed. I feel angry at times when I think about the relatives, teachers, doctors and others who had an opportunity to speak up, question things, and call attention to situations that might point to abuse and neglect at home. I wonder if our societal ability to detect such hidden types of abuse and neglect has improved. Or are there just as many silently suffering children who then grow up to become adults who struggle with jobs, relationships, and their own families?

Not only have I needed to cope with the pain of acknowledging the lack of nurturing and support I needed from my primary caregivers as an infant, child and teen, but I've had to accept that certain coping mechanisms I adapted to this situation harm me, and potentially my other relationships. An overly developed sense of having to shoulder great burdens, do things correctly, take initiative, not share my inner reality, not accept my own weaknesses and limitation, not be open to criticism, and rely too heavily on my own resources: these isolate me from others, even as they were effective in dealing with stress as a child. My husband is concerned that I push myself too hard, take on too much, and am a perfectionist and overly controlling. I need to accept and acknowledge these sides of myself and gracefully let them go, return them to their rightful place – as temporary, stop-gap measures that I over-employed under stress, not as everyday behaviors.

Gain through loss: Losing a mother to become one

"There's no time like the present," is a phrase my mother has always appeared to think meant, "The present has no time." Her emblematic trait is one of permanent non-present-ness. I didn't have the experience or terminology to know how to describe her until I studied Eastern religions, practiced meditation and yoga, lived in Asia for a year, and most importantly, became a mother.

This state of distraction goes a long way towards explaining why I have always felt I didn't have a mother in the sense most of us think of a mother. I had a cleaner, a tender, a bather, an organizer, a planner; but her emotional, psychic presence teetered between extremes of vacuity, and flare-ups of anger and frustration.

When I became a mother, I was presented with the most complex, demanding and important job I have ever had. The depth of instinct and emotion that childbearing and rearing activates, combined with the expansive skill set required to carry out its myriad tasks, meant that I found myself, in addition to grabbing for Sears and other modern day experts' words, reaching desperately back to my childhood role models.

Joy, Interrupted

What has taken me the longest to resolve is the fact that my primary role model, my mother, explicitly rejected her role as a mother. What had previously been a sense of discomfort lurking at the edges of my consciousness, turned into a ton of bricks that dropped on me soon after my son was born. This lonely, scary, painful place drove me to therapy, nearly drove my husband away, strained my friendships, brought me to the brink of major depression, and, in the end, caused me to dig deeper inside than I ever knew possible. In my sleep-deprived state, I experienced a terrifying sense of loss.

As I slipped, tripped and gradually eased my way into motherhood, I vividly re-experienced the loss I felt as a child. More pressing and visceral was the knowledge that I was missing a key support person in my life. She was alive, well, traveling to Europe, volunteering and staying fit, but would forever, just as when I was little, be absent as my mother.

I felt locked out of a club that everyone else was being inducted into as a new mom. Showers, calls, visits, gifts, but more importantly, a caring presence who was concerned about me and thinking about my child as he developed; these were all out of the question. I couldn't answer everyday questions, like, "When is your mom coming down?" or, "When are you going to visit your parents?" without either flat-out lying or sitting down for a two hour heart-to-heart talk.

What I found in her instead was reluctance, ambivalence, uncertainty – the famous distance and disembodiment I had grown up with! She would only visit if I called and asked her to come down, only send things I needed on her own time frame and include no personal note or special touch. There was very little that was spontaneous, heartfelt or caring in her gestures.

After doing research and talking with several therapists, I have tentatively put a label on my parents as a tool for framing a difficult situation so as to gain perspective, delimit their influence over me, and adapt healthier coping mechanisms. This gave me the language to explore the issues during my childhood that had been largely invisible and hard to articulate. The DMR definition of Narcissistic Personality Disorder* seems to me to best fit both of my parents. This cautious diagnosis allowed me to break my sense of isolation and join a community of people with similar experiences and struggles.

This definition also went far in explaining why my every interaction with my mother caused me to re-experience my childhood hurt, pain, and sense of abandonment. If I called her and left a message (always the machine!), I would find myself inexplicably tense for days as I subconsciously clocked how long it took her to call back. After she called, I would be furious about her distance, guardedness, and emotional unavailability as I heard the familiar clanking of pots in the background. I asked in an email once whether it would be possible for her talk on the phone without cleaning at the same time so I could have her undivided attention; she hasn't called since.

With the luxury of distance and time, I often wonder with sadness what events or combination of factors made this first of five siblings lock herself away and feel unworthy of loving herself. I reflect back on her desperate attempts to crack the code to her inner life – the personality tests, the job-preference screenings, and applications to various graduate school programs. None of these led to anything she apparently enjoyed. She herself seemed to be empty, unknown to herself, and in need of someone to guide her.

When I try to put myself in my mother's shoes, and construct a sympathetic narrative to explain her, I do feel it helps to heal the hurt. Born in the booming '50s of the U.S., World Wars, Depressions, and European poverty cast long shadows over her Polish and Irish American relatives. Thriftiness, frugality, faith in God and helping one's neighbors formed a tight small-town ring around her upbringing. The feminism, radicalism, a growing internationalism of tastes and consumer products of the 1960s, occurring when she came of age, encouraged her individual expression. She was involved with more community efforts, peace marches, political activities than could fit on a poster board. The odd part of it is that somehow my mother seemed to think that marriage and childbearing straight out of college would further these aims – perhaps it was the 1950s influence of viewing marriage as a means for not only escaping one's own family of origin, but also attaining individual expression, status, material well-being, self-gratification, and never-ending love.

In any case, the realities of having two children close in age in her early 20s inevitably clashed with whatever romantic notions of marriage she had, not to mention limiting her involvement in the enticing opportunities opening up to women. Her response was to shut down and retreat while she rationed and channeled her energy into the practicalities of daily life. Meanwhile, opportunities passed her by. Initially swallowing her dreams, she then began to chase them frantically when we were a little older. To distance from her kids and dull home life, I remember her frequently on long phone calls, cigarette in hand; and we had regular babysitters while my parents kept up their social life, and regular stays at grandma's during their child-free trips to Europe.

Taking stock, moving forward

How did I emerge from this strengthened, if not also mellowed and tempered?

It's an ongoing, cyclical process. I have had to dredge up and embrace my own grief, while its handmaid's anger and resentment still painfully bubble to the surface and require work. I have to examine my usual modes of behaving and my deep-set tendencies and habitual reactions to situations and people, as these bear the mark of someone who was afraid as a child, who felt unprotected and unloved, and thus undeserving of emotional fulfillment. I've needed to let my hidden self catch up and fuse with the tougher me to form a more mature, steady, and less fearful and anxious adult. Again, I've found often that my own kids, with their present focused energy, can help me slow down and see patterns, and work in these small but important ways to let a more integrated, responsible, and less needy, self emergence.

I've had to talk myself into knowing that my parents have severe limitations as far as what they can give me – and sometimes I still get romantic longings for everything to be magically "alright" and I can almost manage to talk myself out of this. Adopting a more pragmatic approach to daily life also allows me to better manage this emotional maelstrom while I keep focused on my work as a mother.

After a recent disturbing visit to us, for the first time I stated my specific concerns to my parents. After months of them failing to respond to my observations and requests, I calmly wrote to say that while they could write or call the kids if they wanted to maintain a relationship with them, I personally did not want further contact. While I have felt temporarily relieved by this decision, and it has given me the necessary breathing room to grow into a healthier and happier mother and wife, I don't see it as any a sort of final victory or ending point. It is a stopping place along a path, and I need to stay open to what is yet to come.

In touch with a fuller self, I realized there was really no room for me in my parents' lives. Their subtle, yet powerful coercion does not mesh with the new family dynamic I have been carefully, however fumblingly, constructing. The fact that they never did reach out to my kids when I attempted to put the ball in their court, showed me how hollow their words were about loving their grandkids and wanting to get to know them.

Living in another country allowed me to access the lost parts of myself and reintegrate them into my adult life. Despite the romantic sunsets and expansive vistas in tourist literature designed to lure you to escape to an exotic place, what travel does to everyone in different degrees is to bring you face-to-face with yourself. Most of us will choose an organized, group outing over an unplanned, solo experience. The group and a schedule serve to shield us from the harsh exposure of ourselves as we step into the bright, unfamiliar light of a new environment.

As I reflect upon how much I have traveled and gravitated towards unknown situations, I see that this stepping into the void has been an integral part of me coming to terms with feeling so estranged from myself and my family of origin. By putting myself in unfamiliar situations I have reproduced this feeling of alienation; but because I have done it on my own terms, I have created opportunities that allow me to find my way back to myself. In comfortable surroundings, I lose myself and flip into letting others decide for me what I need. In a sense, immersing myself in foreign cultures has been a powerful metaphor for my childhood and has allowed me the opportunity to know myself, trust myself, and become myself. Things not having the same meaning in another culture has allowed me a certain space to figure out what is right for me; as if only against a stark background could I glimpse the faint parts of myself I want to recover.

Though this journey has required confronting past loss, and initiating still further loss, I know that the support and love of people who do nurture me will always be there if I have the courage to seek it out.

I don't need to keep people in my life because of their expectations and needs. I can be an equal partner in my friendships and other relationships. This still can cause anxiety for me, and fear of rejection and hurt. But it is worth it in the end.

This updated definition of Narcissistic Personality Disorder by the American Psychiatric Association is proposed for publication in the forthcoming (May 2013) 5th edition of the Diagnostic and Statistical Manual of Mental Disorders (DSM-5):

The essential features of a personality disorder are impairments in personality (self and interpersonal) functioning and the presence of pathological personality traits. To diagnose narcissistic personality disorder, the following criteria must be met:

A.   Significant impairments in personality functioning manifest by:
  1.   Impairments in self functioning (a or b):

a.   Identity: Excessive reference to others for self-definition and self-esteem regulation; exaggerated self-appraisal may be inflated or deflated, or vacillate between extremes; emotional regulation mirrors fluctuations in self-esteem.

b.   Self-direction: Goal-setting is based on gaining approval from others; personal standards are unreasonably high in order to see oneself as exceptional, or too low based on a sense of entitlement; often unaware of own motivations.

AND

2.   Impairments in interpersonal functioning (a or b):

a.   Empathy: Impaired ability to recognize or identify with the feelings and needs of others; excessively attuned to reactions of others, but only if perceived as relevant to self; over- or underestimate of own effect on others.

b.   Intimacy: Relationships largely superficial and exist to serve self-esteem regulation; mutuality constrained by little genuine interest in others' experiences and predominance of a need for personal gain.

B.   Pathological personality traits in the following domain:

1.   Antagonism, characterized by:

a.   Grandiosity: Feelings of entitlement, either overt or covert; self-centeredness; firmly holding to the belief that one is better than others; condescending toward others.

b.   Attention seeking: Excessive attempts to attract and be the focus of the attention of others; admiration seeking.

C. The impairments in personality functioning and the individual's personality trait expression are relatively stable across time and consistent across situations.

D. The impairments in personality functioning and the individual's personality trait expression are not better understood as normative for the individual's developmental stage or socio-cultural environment.

E. The impairments in personality functioning and the individual's personality trait expression are not solely due to the direct physiological effects of a substance (e.g., a drug of abuse, medication) or a general medical condition (e.g., severe head trauma).

****

These books have helped me along this journey of reconciling my life and motherhood with my experiences in my family of origin:

An Unknown Woman: A Journey to Self-Discovery, Alice Koller
Mothering Without a Map, Kathryn Black
The Way We Never Were: American Families and the Nostalgia Trap, Stephanie Coontz
Trapped in the Mirror: Adult Children of Narcissists in Their Struggle, Elan Golomb, PhD
The Narcissistic Family: Diagnosis and Treatment, Stephanie Donaldson-Pressman and Robert M. Pressman
Fruitful: On Motherhood and Feminism, Anne Roiphe
The Mask of Motherhood, Susan Maushart
Crazy in the Kitchen, Louise DeSalvo

Joy, Interrupted

Skating with Tropes
by Lori Lamothe

You skate in and out of nervous
and I've worn the wrong red socks,
the ones with holes wide enough
for pain to pass right through.
Everywhere around us, confident
children race past in mismatched pairs
and at the center of the ice a girl
spins perfect circles, again and again,
as if she's caught in somebody's TiVO.

Later, I remember how you clung to me
as I tried to push you too soon away,
remember you falling hard onto a surface
that felt like failure. As if on cue
the Zamboni emerged out of its cage—
paraded back and forth across a ring
scratched and scarred with living.

I watched it smooth the past clean
and wished that a metaphor could turn
into something real, if you needed it to.
For a minute it seemed as if it might,
then the ice went on shining nothing but ice
and we stumbled back out onto uncertainty,
skating in a reverse direction this time
without knowing exactly why.

originally published in Literary Mama

20 Questions for My Daughter's Birth Mother
by Janeen McGuire

1. This year my daughter turned 26, the same age you were when you gave birth to her. Do you remember that day, January 4, 1984?

2. I have always told my daughter that you gave her up for adoption not because you didn't love her, but because you did love her. Is this true?

3. Were you in love with your/my daughter's biological father? What was he like? Do you still love him?

4. Our Child Study says that he wanted you to give her up. (My daughter does not know this, please never reveal it to her.) Did you fight him?

5. By Korean standards, was he from a respectable family? Were you? If so, did that make your pregnancy more shameful?

6. Was your passion stronger than any fear of consequences? Why would you have sex, without being married, in a country so unforgiving? Were you fearful that you were not pretty enough or loyal enough or kind enough or smart enough or talented enough or giving enough (my daughter is all of these things) for a suitable man to want to marry you? Or were you simply not compliant? Not obedient? (My daughter is not these things either.)

7. When you discovered your pregnancy, what was the first thing you did? It never crossed your mind to kill her, did it? (I know female babies are still secretly killed in Korea.)

8. When exactly did you run away? Did you feel guilty for abandoning your six younger siblings? And how did you keep your pregnancy a secret? Did you wrap your belly inside a big hanbok? Did you dress as a man? An old woman?

9. How did you manage the confusion of loving the same baby that you were ashamed to bear?

10. Did you ever go back home? Did you ever marry and have my daughter's siblings? Did your family ever find out about your/my child? Did they forgive you? Did you forgive yourself?

11. Does my daughter look like you? Do you have the same straight hair that shines like obsidian and sapphires in the sun? Do you have the same sable eyes that make it hard to see your pupils? Do you have the same hypnotic smile that creates its own light and dents your chin and stops others from breathing? Like my daughter, are you exotic and beautiful, but not to yourself?

12. What were you interested in as a young woman? Fashion? Shoes? Purses? Marriage? Children? As my daughter is… Or were you just too busy carrying out your duties as your parent's eldest daughter, caring for and managing your siblings?

13. Is there anyone else in the family who has epilepsy, who struggles with mood swings, who drinks too much and eats too little?

14. Do you know that inside my daughter's petite body there is some kind of factory that produces so much electricity and kinetic energy you'd think she was possessed? Do you know that out of my daughter's pretty mouth with now perfect teeth come words that are absurdly funny, words that are exquisitely generous, words that are scalpel sharp, words that are always genuine because it is against her nature to be false?

15. What was it like giving birth to a baby you could not keep? What was it like when you handed your/my daughter over to the Child Welfare Society of South Korea? Did your body ache and your throat squeeze shut and your breasts fill with milk? Did she cry? Did you?

16. Did you imagine that if your/my daughter grew up in a white American family that racism would not touch her life? (If so, you were wrong.)

17. Have you ever dreamt of meeting her again? If you could meet her, do you think she would love you more than she does me?
18. Have you ever prowled my dreams, or was that some other Asian woman in the shadows of my sleep?
19. Do you ever wonder about me? Do you ever wonder if I judge you? Or, just feel the deepest form of compassion and gratefulness toward you?
20. Do you ever wonder if I love her enough?

When I miss my kids
by Merrill Edlund

at night
you warm my side of the bed to take away my chills
in the morning
you sing to me of golden daffodils
and memories of green rolling hills
while I curl into a fetal position
gasp for air

Joy, Interrupted

what would i do after a miscarriage?
by Trangđài Glassey-Trầnguyễn

i sat
gazing at the void
life suddenly taciturn
all things impermanent

i sat
looking out at the green garden
the trees burgeoning with fruits,
the branches plump in blooms,
the birds exchanged greetings
the sunlight cried sparkles

i sat
thinking of my child
of the lost opportunities
to care for her, to toil for her
to meet her, even if only briefly

i sat
praying with my husband
for the spiritual and physical recovery
of all mothers
who had suffered the loss of a child
and praying that they
may one day bear full-term children
according to their wish

i sat
thinking about the world
how many lives are counted in days?
why does it have to be that a quarter of fetuses
pass away in pregnancy?

i sat
embracing the pain that chews on my womb
consoling the sorrow that drenches my heart
comforting myself
in the cradle of mourning

i am only a child
crying by herself
having lost a pearl

They Said
by Merrill Edlund

The Doctor in his white arrogance
said
I don't understand why you're so upset

The Nurse in her heavenly benevolence
said
It was God's will

The Mother in her vast experience
said
It happened, get over it

My heart's loss so immense
said
My child is gone

You
Held my sobbing hand
said
We'll have another

Joy, Interrupted

True Story
by Ivan Jim Saguibal Layugan

This is a true story.

It started on an arctic night, one appropriate to the heavy dramas we used to watch in soap operas. For me, it seemed suitable. Tonight, I received news that I passed the editorial screenings and interviews for the student publication of the university. It was something that I've been nervous and babbling about for days; and now that I have it, I cannot wait to relay the news to my family.

It is only when I stepped into the threshold of our home that I realized something is wrong. There are unexpected guests inside that our humble home cannot contain. The lights were eerily golden yellow and melancholy wafted into the air. It was a sight reminiscent of my grandfather's untimely passing three years ago. In the middle of the living room, I saw mom. She is wearing her usual blouse-and-straight-cut-jeans fashion, with her beautiful curls locked in midair. She smiled at me, and that was when I realized everything is really wrong. She was frozen in time, in a frame. And a casket is lying beside her.

My father was the one who caught me as my energy drained with emotion. It was only this morning when they were full of enthusiasm to give my grandparents a small visit in the province. They left in an arresting vivacity that I almost felt sorry for not going, too. It was because I had my final interview for the editorial board that morning that I decided to stay.

Impassively, I reached for my mom in her last resting place. Her eyes looked heavy in the dim and I remembered the many times we have to cry together. We are all what she really has, she would always say. Those eyes were the same gems that watered when my father went home after quitting his job and became unemployed for many months hence. Those eyes, now closed in possession of death, are what looked over me and my siblings from head-to-toe, not missing a detail, before we go to school.

She was always a hands-on mom. Naturally, because she has not taken any jobs since she gave birth to me 19 years ago. She dedicated her life to helping my father bringing up five children—feeding them, caring, educating, loving. But that night, her hands, once soothing and soft, became dauntingly different. It is impossible, I told myself. My mother is the type who leaves things designed and cogent. She won't leave us like this!

"She was hit by a bus," my father choked. And it seems to stop there.

These things and a hundred more came crashing down on me. Tonight, my mom has gone to join the Creator. Maybe her purpose in life is already fulfilled, which she usually says about those who died. What makes it bearable is that she will finally rest her tired bones and that she could guide us from above. What makes it agonizing is that we will be left alone. It's not that my mom left us with no skills or values. She taught us much of that that we can utilize in two lifetimes. She was the family's stronghold. When we all come home in the evening, she is there to ask and listen to each of us. None of us can endure that, not even our father. Our family is not a family without our mother.

The hours ticked away and my father decided I needed to get some sleep. Tears just won't stop pouring but my body cannot argue with my brothers leading me to my room. I rested my head, grave in deep emotions, in the pillow covered with sheets freshly washed by mom the other day. The fabric conditioner made me light, and, in a while, I wondered if maybe everything is a dream. Maybe I can wake up and things will be back to normal. Then I put up a million promises until I faded to sleep: if mom is alive, I won't answer back at her rudely, I will make coffee for her each morning, and I'll wash the laundry for her on weekends, ad infinitum.

106

The greatest miracle: I woke up from that reverie.

My eyes flew open and I realized that real tears are drying in my cheeks. I leaped out of bed and, with no preamble, ran to my parents' room and hugged my mother tight, snuffle mixing with happiness. And just when I thought things could not get any better, my mom quipped:

"Why, you did not make it into the school paper?"

I could have told her that any other things could fail as long as I have her. In a time when things went back to zero, I had her back again and no other accomplishments could equate that.

That was exactly two years ago.

Today, I still get in small fights with my siblings but my mom need not rebuke me anymore, because I give in. I help her in her small business ventures like karinderias (food stalls) and we get closer with everything we do in collaboration. We also do some laundries and chores and I think nothing could replace a bonding like that.

Sometimes, that dream comes back to me in forms of memories. I would never forget how she looked like inside that coffin and I want her to get back the efforts she selflessly gave us—maybe not in figures, but maybe in words like this. I will not waste the seconds ticking by. After all, this is our true story.

Joy, Interrupted

March for Love
by Jenn Williamson

I hear them before I see them, this rag-tag, silly mob
of marchers or stompers or walkers. The arrhythmic drumbeat,

the cheerful whistles and hoots, counterpoint the dusty solemnity
of the university library, and it's impossible to stay on the page.

Outside tinted floor-to-ceiling windows, the first demonstrators
straggle across the red-brick courtyard gleefully stepping and hopping,

an uncoordinated syncopated gait that grooves and moves and stops
to wave at us. Dressed like tinkers or gypsies, they're a variety of bright reds

and greens and yellows, with heart-patterned boxer shorts over sky-blue sweat-pants,
or glitter-heart pop-up headbands and rainbow-striped knee-socks.

They carry signs that read, "March for Love," and I can't tell
if they're celebrating or protesting. Watching the small group move past,

I think of my mom, who is back home getting chemo, probably sitting
in front of tall safety-glass windows in another solemn room, listening

to the even rhythm of the IV machine click and gasp, pushing fluids
into the access port permanently installed in the right side of her chest.

The doctors told her they couldn't put it too close to the heart—too dangerous.
I wonder if they meant the procedure itself, or if it was too risky to dose her

at full strength with medically-approved toxins too close to the organ
that pumps it through her body, filters it down to the cancer cells

blooming in the microscopic recesses of her body. I hate that we have to kill her
and regenerate her a tiny bit at a time. I hate that her body is both enemy and refuge.

One of the marchers seems to be able to see through the tinted windows,
can tell I've put down my library book and am watching the gangly procession.

He smiles at me, waves an invitation. With one hand, he lifts his green bowler hat and bows
like a courtier, then returns it to his head, turns his back, and proceeds swiftly on.

Longing

Come to me in my dreams, and then
By day I shall be well again!
For so the night will more than pay
The hopeless longing of the day.

Matthew Arnold, "Longing"

"Stone Flowers" – Grace Benedict – Colored Pencil on Paper

Depression is the stage I am most comfortable in while grieving. It was my default state after my heart was broken when my daughter died. Like bargaining, it is a longing for something else, but it occurs when we feel that there can never be anything more, nothing else is possible. We are stuck in the state of now and the future seems no more. I see this emotional suspension in Jessica Karborwiak's "Containment."

Rather than identifying this stage as depression, I call it "Longing." It seems the depression stems from this guttural longing I see in Nancy Ruffin's "The Chosen" and the simple wistfulness in Lottie Corley's "Sweet Little One." I associate longing with depression because no matter how deep we go in the dredges of our loss, we long for what had been.

Our intense longings seem to ever persist, as I felt when reading Joanne L. DeTore's "The Dead Woman's Float" and Merrill Edlund's "Leaving earth before you planned." We must learn to accept what is, even though our longings do not go away, as I see in Jenn Williamson's "The Daughter that Lived" and Megan Moore's "Life without Rain." We are depressed because we lost, and it is because of this loss we long. I feel this loss when I read Erin Williams' "Miscarriage" and Svetlana Bochman's "The Best Mother."

Some see depression as the absence of feeling, the absence of desire. But, I think that characterization ignores the intense longing we experience while in this state of inaction. I feel this intensity in Yolanda Arroyo Pizarro's "Hades" and Merrill Edlund's "Kalem."

It takes effort to hope. We must be active to have faith. It is easier to fall into despair and to close our eyes to what has been than what is before us. I see resistance to this fall in Paul Salvette's "A Letter on Srinagarindra Road."

The pieces in this section elicited feelings of longing in me or introduced me to the longings of others. So many reflect a state of suspended being, where nothing can comfort us or replace our loss. I felt this longing when I read Terri Elder's "Ready for Stardust" and "Dreaming as the Summers Die."

In the course of editing these pieces, I recognized my longing and stopped seeing the longing define my life. The longing was still at the edge of every moment, like I felt in Jenn Williamson's "The First Dream," but I was able to learn to have new and different longings, as I felt when reading Pooja Sachdeva's "Remembering the Days Spent Together."

My depression softened as I could move again. My breathing stabilized as my heart opened up for more.

From my perspective, the pieces in this section all reflect some state of suspended grace and intense longing. They show a life paused by grief *and* the possibility of waking from the deep sleep of grief.

110

The Chosen
by Nancy Arroyo Ruffin

They say the child chooses the mother
Before they are conceived.
They search and search until they
Find the perfect place to settle in
Like 1492 Columbus did
In search for a new world.
Yet here I am…
a woman not worthy to
hold the title of mother for
no child has chosen me
to be its home
life sentenced protector~~
Created to breathe life into its lungs
Birth seeds of hope from my ovaries
that will bloom into
a future writer, artist, or world leader
Beauty wrapped up in
golden satin sheets of new beginnings
Carrying within it a shock of ambiguity,
A soul thought up
But undelivered.
Magnificent one, all mine,
A mirror perched
Beyond my reach,
A colossal presence,
you sting with continuity
underneath my skin
You are~
in the hills of my bones
in the apex of my muscles
in the crown of my hair
in the gentleness of my hands
in the waterfalls of my blood
in the light of my shadow
You are everywhere
And nowhere simultaneously
Driven by the restless urge to create
I am inseminated with cultural reminders
of what it means to be a woman.
The woman of the house
Maid to clean,
wash,
cook,
take care of my husband
and when the time comes

111

Joy, Interrupted

bear his child.
But I sit still and wait.
I am a broken clock
that doesn't tick
My time has not come.
I have not been chosen
to miss those cycles
of the moon changing within
My womb weeps blood tears,
the months the shards of grief begin
flowing through me and out of me
iridescent stem of womanhood.
For the sea of faith was too once full
I see you stare back at me
behind an encasement of time.
Not meant to be, not born
Yet omnipresent,
brown-eyed,
laughing,
Above the air I breathe
heavy rain clouds
finally release their pain
ragged currents flow down my cheeks
all of your beauty seen so vividly
I keep your picture in a frame
until the day that we meet again.

Dreaming as the Summers Die
by Terri Elders

"Still she haunts me, phantomwise…"
—Lewis Carroll, *Through the Looking Glass*

I figured something special might be happening that July morning in 1948 when Mama appeared in the bedroom doorway, brandishing her boar-bristled hairbrush in one hand, my not-too-faded red plaid dress in the other.

"Skip the shorts and shirt today," she said, handing me the dress. "Company's coming for lunch."

"Who?" I asked, puzzled. I couldn't think of anybody important enough to wear my Sunday dress for, but I slipped into it, and stood quietly while Mama tugged the brush through my snarls.

I had just turned eleven. No longer in pigtails, I hadn't yet mastered pin curls. So I wore my hair shoulder length and loose around my face, with bangs that forever needed trimming. Maybe I'd learn to set it with bobby pins before I started junior high that fall.

I waited for Mama to answer. "It's Nana," she finally said. "Nana, and maybe Jean." I looked up sharply. Jean was my "real" mother, and I hadn't seen her for years. I glanced across the bedroom at my older sister. Patti and I, just a year apart in age, had been adopted by our "real" father's sister and her husband in 1942, when we were five and six. Patti yawned, and then threw me a wink. Nearly a teen, she was more interested in boys than family gossip.

"Can I go over to Jimmy's?" I asked, as Mama patted my bangs into place.

"Okay. I'll send Patti over to get you when they get here. Just don't get too dirty."

Jimmy lived three doors down and was my best friend. The two of us would climb a towering maple tree to his roof where we would sit for hours, endlessly arguing. I favored the Brooklyn Dodgers and Doris Day. Jimmy loved the Giants and Peggy Lee. I liked Jack Benny, he Fred Allen. Though we rarely agreed, we relished our debates.

A few days earlier we had perched on the roof to watch the July 4 fireworks from the Los Angeles Coliseum. Some evenings we sat up there for hours with Jimmy's telescope, searching for UFOs. We even argued about the merits of the planets. I favored Jupiter, he Mars.

I'd be glad to see Nana, Jean's mother, who always wore sweet gardenia perfume and talked about how she conferred with spirits at her spiritualist church. But I barely remembered Jean. I knew my Daddy Al, of course, Mama's brother, because he visited from time to time. Jean, though, was just a shadowy background figure, referred to in disapproving whispers. She drank, I'd heard. Or she had mental problems, whatever those might be.

She and Daddy Al had married when she was just a teenager, Mama said, and then Patti and I came quickly. Jean just couldn't manage.

More important to me, I knew she was the daughter of a world famous organist, Jesse Crawford, known throughout the '30s as "The Poet of the Organ." Grandpa Crawford sent Christmas cards with photos. I'd heard that he'd had radio shows in Chicago, and was the featured performer at Radio City Music Hall in New York City. My sister had inherited all that musical talent, but none trickled down to me.

"Jean could have been a concert pianist," Mama said once. Jean's brother, Howard, was a musician, too. My taste in music ran more to Vaughn Monroe than classical. *Ballerina* was my current favorite that year. I'd hum it all the time, but wished I could play it on the upright.

113

Not fair, I used to think. I was the one with the middle name, Jean, so I should be the one with the family talent.

Jimmy and I argued well past noon until Patti eventually appeared. "They're here," she announced, with a smirk and a roll of her eyes. I shinnied down the maple, careful not to tear my red plaid dress.

Jean looked younger than I expected, and prettier, with hair the same dark brown as mine, and freckles, just like mine, sprinkled across her nose. But during lunch she never smiled. Not once. Nana talked of the séances she conducted. Mama talked of how Patti and I soon would be starting junior high. Jean just sat, nibbled at her tuna sandwich, glanced about our tiny kitchen, and looked as bored as Patti.

I wanted to ask if she had seen *Easter Parade*, my new favorite movie. I wanted to ask where she lived, if she traveled, if she liked to play Parcheesi or Tripoley. I wanted to ask if she remembered when I was born. Which did she like to read, *Coronet* or *McCall's*?

But soon everybody was saying goodbye. Jean gave Patti and me each a hesitant hug.

"You girls look great," she said, the first words she'd spoken directly to us all afternoon. I wanted to tell her that I liked her freckles, but before I could speak, they were all piling into Nana's Studebaker.

Later that summer, Jimmy's family moved away and I never saw him again. Neither I, nor anybody else in our family, ever saw Jean again either. She just vanished. Nobody ever knew where she had gone. One afternoon a couple of years after that visit, I heard on the radio that my Nana, Olga Crawford, first wife of famed organist Jesse, had died in an apartment fire at the age of 57.

A few years later I sent for my birth certificate, which had been altered when I was adopted, to show Daddy and Mama as my parents. Astonished, I found my middle name was spelled Jeanne, not Jean. Was this how my "real" mother spelled it?

Grandpa Jesse came to my high school graduation and gave me a Smith Corona portable typewriter I had treasured all through college. Throughout the late '50's, I visited him frequently. He hadn't seen Jean since she was in her early teens and was uncertain about how her name was spelled.

I saw Daddy Al from time to time until he died in 1992. He had been married to Jean for such a brief time and so long ago. He had neither their wedding certificate nor divorce papers, so couldn't help me with the spelling.

Across the decades I think of her. Was she Jean or Jeanne? Did she read Hemingway or Fitzgerald? Would she choose pistachio or burgundy cherry if she were at Curries Ice Cream Parlor? Did she ever marry again or have more children? Did I have half-brothers or -sisters that I didn't know about?

Later, at UCLA, I spent a year interning for Los Angeles County Department of Adoptions while I worked on an MSW degree. I learned about the adoption rules of earlier days, about sealed birth certificates and efforts to protect birth mothers. I also learned why many adult adoptees feel an urge to know, a need for answers.

Even now, in my seventies, I'd like to see my original birth certificate. Every time I sign my name, Theresa J. Elders, I wonder if that "J" really stands for Jean or Jeanne. And I still dream about climbing maple trees…and about my mother's freckles.

The First Dream
by Jenn Williamson

Six months after we buried you, you came to me,
and I was vaguely surprised to find myself
in your dream-lit kitchen, standing by the scarred wooden table
that had been moved to my house years ago.
You were seated in your usual place, and we both knew
that you were waiting where you always had been.
Then I was kneeling at your lap, too grown to climb into it,
but not beyond the wish to be rocked and sung to sleep in sleep,
soft as a feverish child, now a supplicant,
my face in the soft press of your thighs, your arms—
somehow—around my body. I remember tears, but not if they were yours or mine or ours,
just the embrace, the holding on, and
the knowing and knowing and knowing.

Joy, Interrupted

The Dead Woman's Float
by Joanne L. DeTore

Nothing is better than hearing your laughter, my girl,
your tiny legs, pumping furiously, dancing like a whirling dervish to the song of yourself.

You grasp my hand in your right hand,
your father's in your left,
and bring us together with your hug,
smiling from ear to ear, believing that your parents are in love
and will be together forever.

I believed it once too. I belicved that we would be different,
laying on that cheap bed in our white trash trailer,
books and papers hidden among the sheets,
empty Chinese take-out on the night stand, reading Donne's sonnets,
discussing the virtues of Cezanne.

I wouldn't have believed it then, laying naked across my then-boyfriend's
chest, legs draped over his, running my finger along his lips.
I wouldn't have believed in things I couldn't see,
that indefinable space that seems to ingest
more of us as we move through our lives.
It swims through me, envelops me before I know I'm struggling for air.
I began sinking on the day I vowed till death do us part,
and now it's official –
the person I was is dead.

I can remember almost nothing from that wedding day
except from pictures, the memories float like photos underwater,
distorted and surreal.
I remember the feeling of drowning
as I approached the church with my father in the black limo.
Like Houdini, I thought I was some kind of escape artist,
submerging myself inside the box with each step nearer to the altar,
until the lid closed completely.
I forgot the key back in the limo.
I imagined a bad soap opera scene,
where the man I loved since I was 14,
burst into the church just as the priest said,
"Is there anyone who knows why these two should not wed,"
and we'd ride away on his motorcycle.
But no one appeared.

I had made my choice.
Settling for second best. I couldn't help but feel sorry for both of us.
I gave what I could, only a part of my heart,
and he gave what he could,

116

a heart of dark secrets.

A beautiful girl and a handsome boy later,
you were life preservers in an endless sea of tears,
keeping me afloat for years.

One day, I surfaced finally, face down, knowing that I drowned long ago
and had only myself to blame.
I threw the rocks out of my pockets,
felt myself rise to the surface.
I swam to the shore with the sun rising on the summer solstice.

You didn't know the old me, full of laughter and promise,
but you will.

Joy, Interrupted

Remembering the Days Spent Together
by Pooja Sachdeva

"Water bag broke." I shouted feeling the adrenaline rush. A beautiful morning after the day when my contractions turned from manageable to unmanageable, I wanted baby to come out. "Baby must want to enjoy more sausages for supper," my husband tried to calm me down. And here, I lie in the hospital with doctors and nurses making a semi-circle around me after my baby enjoyed the dinner. Strong emotions, negative and positive, keep crossing my mind, making me more anxious. Short, quick breaths are helping little to control my nervousness. Going through all this pain, I still am keeping my arms around my belly to protect my child in my womb.

Strange thoughts, odd ideas kept coming in my mind all those months when my mother's stomach grew strangely rounder and rounder. For a few months, when belly protruded little, I thought she must be growing fat. Like a curious little child, when belly took fully rounded shape, I sensed some problem.

"Are you going to leave me?" I asked in my quizzical manner.

And for the first time, my question was answered in a question, which I thought grammatically wrong. She asked, "Do you want a little brother to play with?" Imagination started playing with my mind. Only thought of having an all time partner to play with made me excited to the core; so I replied affirmative.

"I will be back with your brother in few days."

All my colorful imagination turned black and white. I couldn't understand the need of leaving me to get a playmate. So the argument settled when my mom said, "Ok, your brother will be your choice. You come to hospital and pick one you like." The feeling of pride took over me; such a big decision of bringing a member in the family is upon me. I was elated.

"This is the time to push," says a nurse, and I refuse saying, "I cannot, I am not able to." My refusal comes out of my fear, my uneasiness with the surrounding, with the "hospital smell."

"If you don't push, I have to use forceps."

My mind goes blank on doctor's words. I don't want forceps, neither do I want to push.

"Push and we will be proud parents." There is nothing neither new nor magical about what my husband just said, but courage comes over me such that I decide to push and bring the baby out myself.

"Push hard...you have to push hard."

The sound keeps on echoing in the hospital room. My efforts of 49 minutes bring my baby out.

I created life! The thought strikes my mind while tears still keep on rolling over my cheeks. Heavenly peace overcomes my mind, all my fears calmed down as I see my little, pink, crying baby in my arms.

The feeling of pride is same as earlier. Then, I was chosen to decide who would be a new member to our family, and now I am chosen to bring a new creature to life and to family.

Honking vehicles, noisy streets, traffic signals thronged with coconut water sellers, bikes going zigzag to make its way through traffic, overcrowded buses; nobody seemed happy about the decision I was going to make. We managed to reach hospital. Big building, red, white, pink flowers smiling at me, bushy green trees waving at me, tiny birds chirping songs for me; nature was happy about the choice I was going to make, it was in full synchronization. We stepped in the building. The "hospital smell," which is something like my grandmother's perfume, was same. I went in the room, and it was full of cradles. The room was full of babies, I saw getting closer. Some sleeping, some crying, some looking at me thinking I would take them along. The decision was made. I selected a baby.

"We obey you darling!"

Dad took the baby in his hands, and I felt proud. I held him in my arms, caressing him, loving him. My heart is still pounding with joy holding my baby in my arms. My tears promised her that I will protect her always; I will give her all the love and care she wants. My heart pounded once more, this time in grief.

My mother must have promised me all such things, not one of them she is able to make. Small fights are important in love, I have heard. What when fights do not seem to be small anymore?

"This is the biggest mistake of my life," my dad said angrily to my mom.

"If I had known, you would not remain same all these years, I would have left you long before," my mom quipped.

"It has become difficult to breathe peacefully in this house," dad remarked, "and this is all because of you and your habits."

"What did I do wrong to you?"

"What more wrong can you do to this house? The mistake is mine. I brought you to ruin me and my children's lives."

"They are my children too. I have given birth to them."

Boisterous arguments, noisy thoughts, blame games; these had become part of our lives. Though they tried to keep us safe, keeping us in the other room, but the rooms were definitely not soundproof and their noises could easily pierce a wall. My brother was too small to understand all this. I felt chained; I was big enough to understand all that was going on but too small to stop that.

"I want a divorce." That was the height of any argument. "I want to end this fuss," my dad said, "I and my children want to have peaceful life without you." Mom didn't say much that day. Whole day long, I saw her busy packing stuff. The same "black and white" feeling grew in my heart, wondering if she was going to leave us.

"Are you going to leave us?"

"Yes," my mom replied.

My concern and fear rose a level high, and I asked again, "For how many days, mom?"

"Forever."

Monosyllabic answers were sufficient for me to understand the grave situation. Forever seemed too long to me, like some bottomless pit.

"I will go with you." I was firm.

"No, you will have to take care of your little brother. He needs you."

"I need you too, mom."

She ended the conversation saying, "I can't help it."

Next morning, she came to kiss me and my brother good-bye. Her eyes were swollen and red as if she spent her night weeping. I was unable to control my feelings. Just few days, when she had left to bring my brother home, seemed like a nightmare. How could I be able to live without her "forever?" I held her by the leg and wept, and cried, and shrieked, "Don't go mom, don't leave us alone." My cries, my pain fell on deaf ears. A little tender heart was torn. She was gone.

All these years, I questioned her love for me, for my brother, until I myself became a mother. I realized no mother in this world would ever resist loving her child. Loss of motherhood remains the biggest loss, always. She must have felt the pain; her heart must have pounded for us. We never talk about her at home; it makes my dad sad, sad about the loss of 8 years of marriage. I just know that court denied her our custody.

I encountered realities, went face to face with few of them. I left my make believe world the moment I realized that my brother wasn't my choice; he came to us through mom. Hyderabad has a tropical climate which makes its natives dark skinned. We, being natives of northern part of India, have lighter skin. Out of all the children lying and crying in the hospital room, only my brother seemed matching me, so I picked him up, feeling proud about a decision that was not mine.

Things went on from this small early realization. A new mother was welcomed in our home until she decided to treat me like an enemy. I had accepted her as if her behavior with her own child would have been same.

All the bedtime stories that my mom used to tell me seemed real. Fight broke out between my dad and step-mom when I told him about what she is doing with me and my brother. I did not want more trouble for my dad; I never wanted my dad to suffer at the hands of marriage again. So I decided to keep quiet and remained so. My little brother, who is big now, too learned to tackle these situations well. Time made us strong.

My heart is pounding in pain, holding my little one in hands fearing if I would be able to fulfill my promises, if I would be able to love her and be with her forever.

Joy, Interrupted

Leaving earth before you planned
by Merrill Edlund

Life kissed you

your last child barely off your breast

tiny fingers still grasped

there was nothing

you did or didn't do

death beat your bones like back labor

you flailed here and there

wanted to turn out the light

and suddenly like paper whisking in a breeze

no one could catch

you fluttered away

Hades
by Yolanda Arroyo Pizarro

I asked to see Mommy
corporeal
please, bring her back to this dimension
it has been seven years
too many for my tears
I do not want to see her in a dream
or imagine her
I don't want her transparent touch
or at a table of spiritualist mediums
playing Ouija
or recreating her as a hologram
no ghost in the afternoon, please
no talking through some babalawo
Hadēs, and Ἅιδης
reply to my desire
I want to see her for real
I do not ask for peace
or a tranquility island
a breeze for the baby and the donor
solution for my insomnia
my old battle for the marginalized
the elimination of cold at 16 degrees Fahrenheit
my feelings will reach only
my mommy with her yellow eyes
so sweet shoulders prior to levitation
no superficial
Hadēs and Ἅιδης
reply to my desire
I want to see her for real

Joy, Interrupted

A Letter on Srinagarindra Road
by Paul Salvette

The man trudged down the street holding three bags from the market in each hand. His gray factory uniform lay heavy against his shoulders from the rain. Because he only wore sandals, he was mindful not to step in the filthy water streaming into the drains. A taxi raced down the thin road, and he had to step into the mud of a construction site to avoid being hit. While his feet sank into the muck, he noticed a plastic sign hanging on a metal frame announcing there would soon be new condos selling for 2.1 million baht at this location. The dark-skinned workers with rubber boots were resting under tarps, and they chuckled lightly at his misfortune. The man just smiled and kept moving.

He saw the constant stream of traffic heading north as he approached the intersection of Srinagarindra Road. Cars splashed water onto the sidewalk as they zoomed past. On the opposite side of the divided road, massive banners hanging down the exterior of the newly constructed mall advertised a sale on women's shoes until the 15th of June. The man made a mental note to inform his wife when he returned home.

Today, the fruit stall attached to a motorcycle, which was normally set up just before the intersection, was missing. As the man walked around the corner, he noticed that all of the small shops lining this stretch of Srinagarindra Road--selling everything from hardware to insurance—were shuttered. A paper sign taped onto the door of the optical store simply said "Gone Upcountry."

The man realized why no one had wanted to work today at this intersection, and it had nothing to do with the rain. Exactly one year ago, a little girl had died in this exact place.

Typically, the man avoided crossing here because it brought up disturbing memories. However, like most pregnant Thai women, his wife wanted sour mangoes, and the kind she liked were only available at the market down the street. He was exhausted from his 10-hour shift at the factory, and passing through this intersection saved time on the long walk home.

He stood alone at the corner of the intersection, vividly recalling the terrible events. At the time, he drove an ice truck for his uncle and Srinagarindra was part of his delivery route. The two young men, who always rode in the back, wanted to finish the day early because there was a Premier League game scheduled to come on in the early evening. The man had promised them they would get through their deliveries as quickly as possible.

When he had pulled up to the intersection, he edged the truck forward a bit to work his way into the flow of traffic and didn't notice the oncoming motorcycle. Riding the small Honda was a woman in the left shoulder. The man saw the woman grab hard on the front brakes, spinning the rear wheel out of control. Sandwiched between another young woman, there was a small child standing up on the seat, holding onto the handle bar in the back. The man saw the fear in the child's eyes as they were just meters from impact.

The front wheel of the bike ran under the bumper of the man's truck and the woman riding rolled over the top of the hood. The other woman in the back flung onto the pavement, while the little child catapulted directly into a concrete pole that held up a series of electric lines.

Until the ambulance arrived, her lifeless body was trapped in a rat's nest of wiring three meters in the air. At that time, the man was not faulted by the police for this accident because the women had lost control of her motorcycle. However, there wasn't a day that went by when he did not think about the poor child who had her bones crushed when she hit the pole.

As the man's mind drifted into quiet contemplation of what had happened, he noticed a letter floating in a puddle on the sidewalk. He gently pulled it out of the water. It was addressed to "Little Sunisa" in a woman's handwriting. He examined the back and noticed it was a flyer for a variety of sodas at 7-11.

My little Sunisa, what did you dream about it? Did you look to the stars and think about where they were going? You always liked to lay down in my arms and stare into the night sky. I never knew what you wanted, but I think I do now.

My little Sunisa, what did you want to be when you grew up? Your skin was so fair and light, you could have been a movie star. I always wanted the best for you, and I knew you would have a wonderful husband who could take care of you. Everywhere you went people stopped us and wanted to take a picture of you. You were so lovely.

Sunisa, what did you worry about? Did you think that you came from a bad family? Just because your father left you before you were born doesn't mean I didn't love you. Everybody loves a girl who can come from hardship to become to a star. I'm sure you would have been famous if you had the chance.

Sunisa, do you ever miss me? I know I wasn't the best mother, because I drank and smoked. I may have bad habits, but you always have my heart. You could have learned from my mistakes and become a wonderful woman.

Little Sunisa, are you mad at me? I moved back to Chonburi with my parents after the accident, and I'm sorry I didn't come back until now. It was just so difficult for me.

Love,
Mom

After the man finished reading the letter, he placed it back down in the puddle. An elderly woman sat drinking a bottle of water from a straw behind a locked metal grate in front of her shop house. She stared at him with vacant eyes. He bowed his head slightly, and she grunted with a wave of her hand and pointed her head toward the ground. He looked down the road and walked away. He had to return home with the bags from the market for his wife and children.

Joy, Interrupted

Kalem
by Merrill Edlund

I used to keep you

in the cradle right beside my bed

arms length

breath in sync with mine

now you are a day ahead of me

far away

arms extended

Life without Rain
by Megan Moore

My first baby was born sleeping at 37 weeks and 2 days on October 20 2007. Her name is Rain Serenity Arizola. Rain was born sleeping due to Intrahepatic Cholestasis of Pregnancy. ICP is a pregnancy related liver condition in which there are abnormalities in the flow of bile. The abnormalities in the flow of bile lead to a buildup of bile acids in the mother's blood.

The day I lost my Rain changed my life forever. I am not nor will I ever be the same person or even close to that same person I was. I was 21 years old when I lost my Rain. Since I was young I got the "It's ok, you're young, you can have more kids." I also got, "Well, you had a baby so at least you know you can conceive and hold a baby to term."

Who cares that I can have more??? No one can ever take the place of my baby and just because I got pregnant once doesn't mean I can for sure get again let alone hold a baby full term. The insensitive comments, that didn't even matter, kept coming and coming-- even though I just lost my baby.

I turned straight to God when I lost my baby. I was always a religious person but never really close to God. I really took most things for granted. I only prayed occasionally; but that all changed. After losing Rain, I turned completely to God. I would read the Bible every day, pray every day, and most importantly, I try to live my life in a much better way to please God. I also don't take anything for granted.

I still do ask, "Why my Rain?" and I struggle with knowing she is in a better place but still wanting her here with me. Three and a half years later, I honestly just think this gets harder in time. But, I do make Rain a part of everything our family does and that does make it easier for me.

I have a beautiful website for her on last-memories.com where everyone can light her virtual candles and leave pictures and messages for her. It's a great thing because it helps me know people remember my Rain and are thinking of her. I have met some of the greatest people on this website. A lot of these people have become like family.

I also go to her special spot (the cemetery) almost every day. It's always decorated for every holiday and just everyday stuff. Her spot is never undecorated. We do celebrations for her and the other angel babies and children we have come to know throughout the years. We do balloon releases as well. We always celebrate her birthday at her special spot, we actually bring tables, chairs, food, cake, presents, cards and of course lots of decorations and balloons. There is not that much we mothers can do for our kids who aren't here with us, so I try to do whatever I possibly can do.

In a tragedy you really find out who your real family and friends are. I have cut a lot of people out of my life, but have also gained some new great people in my life. You find out who you count can on.

As a mother who has lost her child, I feel guilty everyday from the day we lost her. I feel like I should have known the doctors were no good and I should have gone to another hospital. I should have done more research on the hospital I was at and the symptoms I was having. I shouldn't have trusted the doctors. Since the loss and since I've had more kids, I feel guilty for not doing enough for my Rain. Nothing seems enough because she is not here with us. We can't take her out to all the kids places or on vacation. We can't buy her a closet full of clothes. There is so much we as mothers can't do for our children who aren't here.

People treat parents who have lost their children, especially babies, wrong. A lot of people won't talk about our children who aren't here, but go on and on about their children, and to a lot of us moms, that's just plain rude. We want you to talk about our children. We want you to help keep their memory alive. There is not enough out there for us parents who have lost their children and there needs to be. My two biggest goals since I lost my Rain is to raise awareness for ICP and baby loss in general and of course keep my Rain's memory ALIVE.

In the beginning, I was full of sadness and anger. I still have anger now and get angry a lot, but I try to always think of the positive now: my Rain is in Heaven with God and will never have to deal with the evil and bad of this world. I have and will grieve everyday; I will never ever get over my daughter. It is not a deep depression type of grieving but a grieving that my world will never be complete. I will never be completely happy my daughter isn't here.

There is nothing that can compare to the loss of a child. We mothers will never be the same without one of our children.

The Daughter that Lived
by Jenn Williamson

Sometimes it's a too heavy
burden, this life—
these un-asked for, livings.

You had a sister who died
three days after she was born,
not your twin, but close enough

to shadow you, the only girl, now,
among four children. She was
beautiful. You wanted to be

beautiful, too. It's hard
to think of you, now, waiting
in a paper hospital gown,

the sage-colored walls
of your tiny examination room
growing smaller and more square
while you wait for the doctor
to tell you that the cancer in your ovaries
will kill you soon,

but you can't think of soon,
so you think of me, and the life
that you want your daughter

to live, to not stop because
of a green room and square walls
and the cold, uncertainty of your unfamiliar body,

because there is no stopping,
and there is just this body,
so you think of me, moving forward,

walking through dry leaves,
one hand pulling my sweater closer,
the other reaching toward the thick, woolen air.

Joy, Interrupted

Ready for Stardust
by Terri Elders

Nobody can do for little children what grandparents do.
Grandparents sort of sprinkle stardust over the lives of little children.
--Alex Haley

I don't think of myself as a crybaby, though I've whimpered at weddings. Oh, all right, I've sobbed at funerals, and sniveled at graduations. Who doesn't? And, of course, everybody cries at sad movies. Why, I recall once dispatching an annoyed boyfriend to the restroom for tissues when I couldn't stop bawling at the conclusion of "Carousel."

But when tears trickled down my cheeks in the foyer of St. John Romanian Orthodox Church, everybody in attendance cast a curious glance my way. I mean, who cries at christenings, aside from infants? I felt relieved when baby Kendra obliged with some howls when she was plunged into the baptismal basin, grateful that she'd diverted attention from me. I fished in my purse for a handkerchief to blot my cheeks dry. My step-granddaughter and I had wailed for different reasons. I suspect she just felt cold, while I felt...old.

I'd never expected to become a grandmother, least of all in my seventies. My son, an only child, while still in his teens had told me he didn't anticipate being a dad. A decade later he married a woman who shared his doubts about offspring. The two happily raise cats.

I'd adjusted to a grandchild-free life easily. As a therapist I'd worked for years with infants and toddlers so hadn't missed out on singing lullabies or reading "Curious George." At high school reunions when former classmates shuffled through photos of grandchildren, I'd nod politely as they bragged about how beautiful, brilliant and perfectly behaved all their descendents turned out to be.

I'd talk about my dogs, and pretend not to see pity fill their eyes when they realized I had no grandchildren of my own.

Then, in my sixties, I met and married a man who had enough grandchildren to fill my calendar pages with birthday reminders. Unfortunately, they all lived half a continent away. I felt a few jealous pangs when girlfriends talked of taking their granddaughters to see "The Nutcracker," or out for banana splits. Nonetheless, I admitted that babysitting grandkids probably wouldn't be something I'd really relish.

Occasionally we'd see the kids at a family gathering, a graduation or a wedding. My husband claimed he didn't know how to relate to the younger ones, though.

"I never know what to say when I see them," Ken complained. "I can play chess with the older ones, but what in the world do you say to a five-year-old?"

I laughed. "Just invite the child to tell you a story. A five-year-old always has a tale to tell, even if it's just a rehash of 'The Three Bears.' You'll see."

Ken looked doubtful. I noticed that the next time we saw his grand kids, one or two blinked up at him with shining eyes. He'd smile for a minute and then turn away. Still uncomfortable, he didn't ask them to tell stories. Maybe he wasn't interested in hearing about Goldilocks. Though the children called me Grandma Terri, they didn't linger near me for long. I guessed they figured I was just a granny-come-lately, not a real grandma at all.

Then Kendra came along. Ken's middle son, Rick, married in his forties, and his wife, Angela, gave birth last year just weeks after my husband succumbed to cancer. This blessed child was his namesake. At eight months she already had her grandpa's twinkling blue eyes and lopsided smile.

I traveled to Arizona for her christening. I couldn't stop grinning when Rick introduced me to the priest as the grandmother. It was just a few minutes later that it struck me that this baby would be my own bona fide grandchild. I started to plan how I'd get to play with her whenever I could get down to Arizona or lure her parents to Washington. I'd remember every birthday, every Christmas. That's when my grin turned into a grimace and I burst into tears. I'd suddenly realized I wouldn't live long enough to snivel as she graduated from high school. I wouldn't be around to whimper at Kendra's wedding.

I finally pulled myself together. I didn't need to worry about the distant future. I could seize each chance to "grandma" as it came. I could send toys and games and books and cards. I could post photos on my Facebook page. I could display the holiday cards I'd get, addressed to "Grandma." I could bore my friends at high school reunions with tales of her antics.

After the christening, one of Ken's old friends approached. "Were you crying because you missed Ken?"

"Yes," I admitted, crossing my fingers.

It was just a little fib, a little white lie. I missed my husband.

Certainly I wish he'd been there with me. But in my heart I knew I cried for all those lost years where I'd never had a chance to sprinkle stardust over grandchildren's lives the way my own grandmothers had over mine.

She's just turned one, but Kendra better watch out. Stardust will be drifting her way soon. I'm prepared to baby sit. So she'd better be prepared to see "The Nutcracker," and to eat banana splits. When she gets a little older, I'll rent a video of "Carousel" and we can sniffle together. In the meantime, she can tell me stories. After all, I've waited far too long to find out what happened to Goldilocks.

And though I'm not a crybaby, she shouldn't be surprised if I tear up a little when I give her a welcome hug…or more than a little when it's time to kiss her goodbye.

Joy, Interrupted

Miscarriage
by Erin Williams

The amniotic sac had ruptured and
run down my legs
Early the day before.
Now in dim fluorescent light
A sudden spasm pushed my twelve week old pregnancy from my body.
The Dr. asked
"do you want to say goodbye?"
Her voice was soft
Her thin, veiny hands
Cradled the partially formed legs and arms
Of my baby.
(It already looked so much like a baby!)
I reached out-
I wanted to grab the little body
And rock it
And kiss it
And push it back inside of me.
I bent my pointer finger,
In a tiny farewell.
And the sobs exploded from my lungs
And my heart pooled around my ankles.

An Anthology on Motherhood and Loss

The Best Mother
by Svetlana Bochman

Dark tunnel of loss
Tunnel of my womb
A baby came through it
But never saw the light

You stopped breathing
Trapped by a bloody clot
My blood killed you
As my blood made you

Sarabeth,
I never knew how much I loved you
Until I lost you-

I longed for you,
Thought I was ready for you
But somewhere between heart and womb
Something went wrong…

How long did you suffer
Struggling to breathe?
When you came out you were all black
With the cord wrapped around your neck
My link to you killed you

They put you in a dress and cap
Like the baby I was meant to have
But you were not yet ready for this world
As I was not yet ready for you

Where do the lost children go?
You are buried in an unmarked grave
With a piece of you remaining in a test tube
For further investigation

Sarah – I'm sorry
I never stopped to listen to your heart beat
Never slowed down enough
To appreciate your kicks
Instead, *I* kicked in protest
At the imposition you were making on my life

I never knew how much I loved you
Until I lost you –
My mind latched on to superficial things

133

Joy, Interrupted

Afraid you wouldn't latch on to my breast
But now my milk is dry with no child to latch on

Dearest child,
I was afraid I wouldn't be a good mother
And then you died
And now I am sure I will be the best

The best mother
Is one who has lost a child…
She truly knows
How much her baby is worth
And knows her own worth
After coming through that tunnel
Holding that infant to the light

Containment
by Jessica Karbowiak

At nineteen years old, I become confused in my body and have to leave college. I walk in padded slippers and ratty bathrobe down the front hall of my childhood home. I avoid my mother and father, my younger brother visiting from college who seems to be avoiding me, too.

I work hard to control myself, my thoughts, my face as I shuffle slipper in front of slipper, reach the dining-room-turned-recuperation-bedroom, slide the glass doors roughly open, enter and close. There is little besides my old black sleigh bed brought in for the occasion and I push my body onto it, crouch in a ball and touch my stomach with both hands until sleep comes.

When I wake, confusion takes over. This becomes the New Normal, thoughts moving over-fast so it is hard for meaning-making to catch up. Weekday and weekend, day and night, what counts and what doesn't. Today is a Friday I know, have been told by my mother several times. My mother, who paces the kitchen nights adorned in her own ratty robe and slippers, paces there in the room next to mine so I cannot help but listen, eyes trained on the ceiling and hands cupped over ears, counting my breaths, feeling guilt and shame until she stops.

I know Friday because tomorrow is Saturday, my appointment at the clinic, the beginning of ending this confusion. I wish for the rest of the afternoon and night to pass quickly even though it's maybe wrong to wish this, maybe I am callous for rushing this ending, but really endings are sometimes beginnings, depending where you start from. At the time I'm okay with the rush, the hot welling-up-in-throat feel to get things over with, move beyond them into something, anything else. I'm okay with possibly being wrong because already I've been wrong in big ways, God knows.

When I leave my bed, it is only to use the bathroom or sit at the family computer to play solitaire. I sit for hours staring at the movement of cards, line upon line and ordered. My sick pit of stomach feels over-empty and over-full in the span of a few minutes, so I shove saltine after saltine into my mouth to stave off the morning nausea, let crumbs build up on the front of my robe.

There is too much noise in the house on the Friday before the Saturday I have my procedure. The click of the computer mouse, the crinkle of the plastic cracker wrapper, the thud of the front door and heavy footsteps up the hall and into the kitchen as my father brings plastic bags filled with items from the list to my mother waiting there; vitamins, thick cotton gauze strips, new pillows, a heating pad. I shuffle unblinking into my parents' bedroom, shove my right hand into the back of my father's nightstand, grab a handful of his construction earplugs—individually wrapped in neat plastic squares—and stuff a pair into place like I always do when the noise of the world blares. The spongy neon orange material fits to the shape of my ear canals. Instant relief and I barely hear the telephone ringing, the whisper of talk between my father and mother in the kitchen as I shuffle back to my bedroom and close the door on the sound.

The summer I was ten years old, I began helping my mother in her garden. It was quiet, just the two of us, kneeling in throw-away jeans, cupping gloved fingers around interloper weeds to pull. We raked up left-over leaves from the fall season, all curled and blackened edges, lifted piles of garden debris into black outside pail, overflowing.

My mother dropped and covered seeds, watered lightly, so lightly it was almost not-watering. A few drops. I heard the heaviness of my father's work boots coming down the back stairs, lifting the pail full of our labor with one strong arm, moving to the side and front of the house without a word.

I collected the cucumbers for pickling, twisted them off vines with one sharp tug and dropped them one after another into a small basket. My mother's body bent down into an L shape to reach the ground, and she wiped sweat from her brow with dirtied glove, left bits of soil and seed there. She rubbed her hands vigorously between the seeding of different vegetables, and they cramped and ached with effort. I helped but mostly I watched, leaned against one of the wire garden rails in my ripped jeans and faded t-shirt, listened to the barely-there sound of singing birds, a faint lawnmower, felt the gentle warmth of sun stream on my bear arms.

After showers and fresh clothes, we stood together at the kitchen sink, rinsing big glass jars brought in from the garage, letting the soap and water swirl in and out, the dust and faint pickling smell from last year removed. My mother showed me how to pickle many times though I never paid attention, don't remember anything really except the quiet talk; the way her knotted, strong fingers cut cloves of garlic quick and light, how I lifted my wide brown fingers to my tearing eyes and marveled at her work.

I knew my mother didn't really expect me to help. My real job came after, shutting tight the lids and placing the full jars in the refrigerator with a grin. Some nights later, I used a fork to fish out a pickle for each family member, passed them around the tiny oval table, taking pride in this tiny contribution as we each let the warm juices flow down our chins. After the season passed, I was responsible for the washing out and thorough drying of the jars, the stacking on garage shelves until next season when the first cucumber grew into the shape of a small comma, and I ran down the front steps and hoisted open the garage door, carried each glass jar gingerly, one at a time, into the kitchen to my mother's waiting hands.

Time jumbles and it is Saturday. I perch on the tippy-tip edge of a cold hard chair in the clinic's waiting room. I read blurry-eyed the mandatory paperwork, walk to the front desk and wobble signature out on line's edge in the smallest script. I follow a no-name woman into a small dressing area where I don a cloth gown open from ass to elbow, feel foolish at how I notice the soft gush of air tickling skin, wish for someone beside me so I can make a dirty joke to push through this moment. Instead, I walk flat-footed across tiled floor, follow the woman between swinging doors, onto table, feet in stirrups, eyes closed. She asks me something but all I hear is static, too loud, and I swallow down the desire to fling myself out of the curtained third-story window, feel the hard crunch of foundation press into my body, the solid there. She says something else and I bite down on my lip and look away. I've learned to ignore words, learned it's dangerous lately to speak, to think, to write anything, anything at all.

It is at least ten minutes before the doctor enters. He is fat, very fat and his glasses are slightly askew. He looks unkempt and there are several dark-colored stains on the front of his gown. I shut my eyes, feel how my legs are open wide, so wide that when the panic comes, I think of how exposed I am and want to laugh out loud, maybe snort a little, though this is inappropriate and confusing because of what I'm here for.

When I look again, there is a light-eyed anesthesiologist beside me. He touches my hand and speaks in soft tones. As I count down from ten to nine to eight, I train my dark eyes on his, let the look and sound of his kindness guide me.

When I wake in the clinic's recovery room, stark white linen chafes my skin. My eyes well up like a child's, perhaps completing my transformation from wronged woman to ravaged thing, staring up at the fluorescent ceiling light.

I notice the flimsy brown knapsack beside my bed, the one I brought with me that holds my wallet, an extra pair of underwear and sweatpants. I feel over-tired and desperate, and my eyes seek out someone to beg for quiet, though I'm not sure where the noise is coming from, only that it overpowers.

A nurse stands by my bedside, asks how I am feeling but all I hear is static, the noise of her, and I wish for a pair of my father's earplugs or the stillness of my mother's garden. I can almost see the pickling jars stacked in the garage arranged by size, know somehow in this moment I should have taken one with me, washed it off with outside hose, the one with the broken nozzle and hardly any pressure. I should have stuffed the lidded jar into my knapsack, settled it among the soft of clothing there, walked stiff and slow through the house, through the clinic as if the bag held only what was asked, as if the bag weighed nothing, next-to-nothing. I see the mouth of the nurse still moving, and I try to reach her across the static.

Do you, is there some way that I can keep it?

An uncomprehending look. Puzzled eyes.

What do you need, hon? What is it you want?

I know this sounds crazy, and I swear I'm not crazy, but can I take it home?

Take what home? The gown?

No, I mean take it home. What the doctor took. I think I'd like to take it home.

I try to explain how this is not a problem, how it is not that weird really, not crazy at all, I have my own jars for this. This makes sense in the moment though the nurse gives me a Concerned Look, nods for another nurse as I cup my hands to my ears at the racket because all of a sudden I realize I am not alone here, there are other women in this room, sick and getting-sick women. We are laid out in two parallel rows, five beds by five, and the sound of coughing and vomiting pushes past the static. More pills, light and fitful sleep and when I wake again, it is hard to breathe so I tighten my whole body, focus one-two-three on my breaths. For a while, this becomes the only important thing.

I stare at the two sets of beds lining the room. They make me think of vegetable rows in my mother's garden as I wait for the doctor's permission to leave, think of my mother probably idling her car in the parking lot by now, waiting and worrying. Later, I am covered with a homemade quilt in my recuperation bedroom when the cramping comes, not plural really, but a single elongated cramp wracking my body so who I am and what my body is capable of no longer seem real or trustworthy. The cramping finds me unprepared, even though I was told about the possibility of this, so when I hear the grunting and gasping of an animal it takes me a while to connect these noises to myself.

The sound of me is loud and long, loud enough to bring my quiet father from the kitchen where he sits nursing a cup of coffee to stand outside my bedroom door. I see his shadow beneath the door, sense his hesitation to enter, to offer me something because whatever he has to offer cannot help, not really, and we both know this.

I yell for my mother though the noise hurts my own ears, scream her name in guttural and strangled tones until my father slides open one of the doors in fear though I ignore his presence, his maybe-shame at my shame, and yell *I'm fine I'm fine it's gone now it's over*, and I wish for my mother so hard it is the only thing that is myself amid this new no-growth and pain. I close my eyes, see my mother kneeling amid garden's green, though it is winter now, the confusion I feel helps this make sense. I see her calloused fingers, no manicure there, wish for those fingers to rub my forehead, my face and shoulders, the move and rub of a knowing mother keeping watch at my bedside like she kept watch over her garden, thumbing out pests and nursing life.

My voice is hoarse now from the calling and my father's face registers shock as need contorts my face, I am still calling and she is here, finally here. She has come home from the pharmacy with my pain prescription, drops all to the floor and lies down beside me on the bed, rubbing the no-growth, the confusion and the pain away. She tends me as my father slides the glass doors closed and retreats to the kitchen, and the only sound now is the soft whisper of my mother's voice to soothe, the gentle scratch of her skin on my skin, and I am no longer a ravaged thing, a shamed and guilty thing, but a living thing, a trying-to-be-alive-again thing, and I let the quiet of her hands do this work. I let her so I can rest.

Acceptance

I hold it true, whate'er befall;
I feel it, when I sorrow most;
'Tis better to have loved and lost
Than never to have loved at all.

Alfred Lord Tennyson, "In Memoriam"

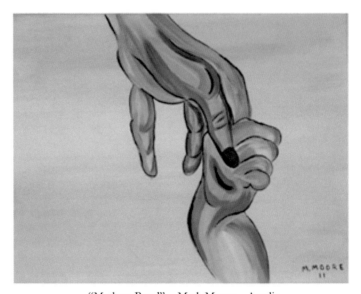

"Mothers Bond" – Mark Moore – Acrylic

Acceptance is a hard concept for the grief-stricken to wrap their heads around. Acceptance implies agreement, which none of us feel after a loss. But, I like to think of acceptance as a type of acknowledgment or awareness. The earlier stages of grief are all coping mechanisms for us to be able to survive--we cannot face the full force of our losses, particularly those that are traumatic, without some sort of denial, bargaining and anger.

I compare the early stages to how we can face intense physical pain, such as in child birth. We can distract ourselves, not bringing our full attention to the pain. We can scream in agony, the psychic energy damping the pain. We can plead to God to help us through the pain. We can tell ourselves, if we just get through the pain, we will do something differently in the future. We can agree to take the medicine, avoiding the pain altogether.

Some of the pain management mechanisms are healthier than others. Some of them work some of the time and we have to use at certain points in order to cope with the pain. Some of the ways we manage pain have certain unintended effects in our lives that can cause more pain for ourselves or others. Some of us get stuck relying on one of these approaches and know no other way to deal with pain.

But another option natural birth advocates and proponents of meditation advise us is that we can *breathe* through the pain. After we have experienced the pain, they tell us, we will feel a sense of accomplishment. The memory of the pain will fade because of the joy we feel after the reward of a bringing a new life into the world. We feel a peace after breathing through the pain. After the pain, we appreciate the important things about life.

But, the hardest thing to believe during such intense pain is that it will stop. This is where faith and hope come in. In the earlier stages of grief, faith and hope are casualties. We hobble along in our "no," our furies driving us, our pleas unanswered. Our coping mechanisms keep us in the dark, perhaps helping us to avoid the pain, distracting us from it, diverting our psychic energy from it, but never really breathing the pain in...and then out.

The pieces in this section all either reflect this breathing in and out of pain, or elicited this reaction in me while I was reading them. This acceptance isn't all light and cheeriness. Some of it is dark and bloody and not for the faint of heart. Some of it is like ripping a bandage off. Other times the breathing is muted, shallow, and struggling. But in all, I felt faith and hope floating back to the top of my consciousness. I was more aware of my own pain than ever, but I was breathing through it.

I don't know if readers will feel the same in the reading the pieces in this section. I am not sure if it was really the pieces themselves that moved me closer to acceptance or if it was because of the point in my journey of grief I happened to be in. But, it is my hope for everyone that reading through the pain, and seeing how others move through the sludge of pain in some of the pieces, will bring us closer to the faith that joy is only interrupted, but never lost.

Loving Benjamin
by Gail Marlene Schwartz

Part Five: Beginning

His eyes are dark and warm, like hot chocolate, and his movements are punctuated and full of life, like a baby Charlie Chaplin. His new lips feel strangely capable on my nipple.
His gaze meets mine and I whisper "well hello, Benjamin," my voice grainy from the surgery.
I nurse him hello and I nurse him goodbye. I haven't seen him since.

Part One: Another Beginning

"Congratulations!"
I listen to the message three times to make sure it's real. Finally, I drop the phone and bolt out the door, barefooted, running to find Lucie, who is walking the dog, and shouting, "We're pregnant! We're pregnant!!!"

Part Two: Waiting and Weighing

Our first ultrasound happens at eight weeks. The tech rubs jelly on my belly and a tiny pulsing heart appears on the screen.
And then, another.
Two bodies. Two heartbeats.
At home that evening, we celebrate with flowers, two yellow mums for them, a white for Lucie and a purple for me. We light candles, hold hands and weep with joy.
I step on the scale. 161. No gain yet.
Our doctor gives me screening tests at week twelve. Afterwards she sits us down; she's concerned about the Nuchal Translucency test, which indicates that Baby B has a one in three chance of having Down's Syndrome. She strongly recommends an early amniocentesis, which would be definitive; "I could do it tomorrow," she says. 95% of women who get this news choose abortion, she tells us, and if it's necessary, sooner is better for the healthy twin.
I am numb and cannot speak.
We finally take an appointment for the amniocentesis in a few days to give ourselves time to think. I cry silently in the car going home, wiping my cheeks and nose with the gray fleece of my jacket.
During the next few days, I think about my fantasy children. One girl and one boy. Talented and smart. Musician and cartoonist. Successful. People who other people cherish. People who care for the world and make me proud.
Of course, neither of these children has Down's Syndrome.
Retarded. Slow. Special needs. Mentally handicapped.
Somebody who 95% of people choose to abort.
No, this news does not fit into my plans at all.
Suddenly I am deeply ashamed. I want to tuck myself into the corner, under the loose floorboard in our bedroom, where nobody can see me.
Lucie and I talk for hours. We already feel like parents and realize that abortion is not an option for us. Our research tells us that Down's babies are easily adoptable by families who feel called to raise special needs kids.
I step on the scale. Again and again and again.
165
165
168

My brain does somersaults around the one in three odds. 66% of the people who get this news have normal kids, I reason. Medical doctors are such alarmists. Two out of three, two out of three, two out of three.

I see a new mom pushing her twins in a double stroller down the street. I turn around and cover four extra blocks to avoid her.

171

172

174

We do it up for Halloween. We spend hours on our costumes, Lucie, a witch and me, the Headless Horseman. We make an orange themed dinner for friends, light candles, and carve intricate pumpkins with the help of Martha Stewart.

172

175

175

I feel my capacity for closeness shut down, like a trap door, and I sink deeper and deeper into darkness.

I think of my own mother, just 22 at my birth. An unplanned pregnancy, I wasn't the child she imagined, either - a beautiful, feminine girl who would play quietly with dolls, do as she's told and take good care of Mommy.

Daily life with her was terrifying.

What if she had given me up?

175

176

175

Part Three: Moving Through the Middle

The doctor calls with the results of the amnio. Baby B has Down's Syndrome.

The waiting is over.

I spend the day with Lucie. We cry and hold each other as we wander through the house. I look for something to fill myself with: flax toast with peanut butter, semi-sweet chocolate morsels, Lucky Charms Cereal with rice milk, a Granny Smith and some cheddar.

The gaping hole remains in the depths of my pregnant belly.

In the evening, I make the mistake of calling my mother. She listens silently for a moment before speaking. "You're not going to KEEP it, are you?" I hang up quietly and lie down on the couch and stay there, staring at the window, until morning.

We talk at breakfast before Lucie leaves for work. We know deep in our hearts that we cannot provide for Baby B. Our advancing ages and my career are reasons enough; I don't even have to fully face my initial shame.

179

177

178

I float out, further and further from my tribe. I am too broken to manage others' reactions, judgments, even their clumsy kind offers of "can I do anything to help?"

179

180

180

I spend more and more time in bed.

Part Four: (re)Birth

Quietness. Emptiness. Agony.

My belly pushes out, more and more, and I sleep in short spurts. My maternity pants keep falling down and I can't walk to the corner without feeling breathless.

We find out they are two boys and decide to name them: Baby A is Alexi, our son. Baby B is Benjamin. We use their hospital initials to honor their time as twins, kicking, elbowing and hiccupping inside me.

182

183

184

Between week 32 and 33, the adoption proceedings begin: we shed tears of relief to find out there is a family waiting for little Benjamin.

Repeated questions about us being sure of our decision are difficult, though.

We are sure...and we are sad.

185

187

187

Occasionally I am still overtaken by fear. "What's wrong with the other one?" "What if something happens at the birth?" "What if I am a terrible mother?"

I feel kicks and see elbows and heels glide across my middle so I focus there. The fear retreats into the shadow of the miracle and starts loosening its grip on my soul.

190

191

192

Part Five: Beginning, again

At 36 weeks, my doctor tells me I am having light contractions and that Benjamin's heart rate is dropping dangerously with each one. She suggests going ahead with an induction, knowing how important a vaginal birth is to me. "We can always wheel you across the hall to the OR for a C-section if there's any problem." I look at her, puzzled. "But couldn't Benjamin die quickly with stronger contractions?" She just looks at me, and finally shrugs. I realize then that my doctor is thinking only of Alexi. She is willing to sacrifice Benjamin, seeing him like most of the outside world will see him. My mind runs through all of reasons C-sections are bad for babies; this is not how I want my son to enter the world. But at that moment, I am Benjamin's mother too, his birth mother, and my job at that moment is clear. I make the decision and the nurses began prepping me for surgery.

I tell our doula, Leslie, and the hospital staff that I do not want to see Benjamin at all after the birth; I need to focus on Alexi and not get bogged down in grief.

Frightened and shivering, they wheel me into the OR in my gown. I am given several medications in my spine and slowly sensations in my bottom half fade away. Lucie comes in after about 15 minutes and holds my hand. At some points I am losing so much blood that I am certain I'm going to vomit. Finally they pull Alexi out and I hear him wail. The nurse puts him on my chest for a few moments before whisking him away to be cleaned. They take Benjamin out next and quickly bring him elsewhere.

When we arrive in the recovery room, both babies are there: it seems the doctors had forgotten my request. A nurse takes Alexi away for some extra oxygen and Benjamin remains in his little plastic bassinet, quietly smacking his tiny lips together. Leslie comments casually that he wants to nurse. I throw caution to the wind, take him in my arms, and give it my best effort: my first moment of breastfeeding. He latches on and nurses like a pro, all the while maintaining eye contact.

His eyes are dark and warm, like hot chocolate, and his movements are punctuated and full of life, like a baby Charlie Chaplin. His new lips feel strangely capable on my nipple.

His gaze meets mine and I whisper "well hello, Benjamin," my voice grainy from the surgery.

I nurse him hello and I nurse him goodbye. I haven't seen him since.

Born to Run
by Emily Polk

The first time I see Indira, really see her, after Jake finally gets permission to wheel me into the NICU, it is near midnight. She is on her back, naked except for a tiny diaper, a purple wool hat on her head, her chest rising and falling in quick little spurts, the pink skin of her body translucent, and broken by a series of thin, fragile blue veins. She is kept warm by the heat inside the glass incubator. There are what seem to be a few dozen tubes and wires sticking out of all parts of her tiny three and a half pound body. Across her face, a ventilator helps her to breath. Tomorrow we will take her off the ventilator and hold her while she dies.

Her heart will not survive the surgery she needs to repair it. But in this moment, this first moment of seeing my daughter for the first time, my only thought, when I can catch my breath against the wave of enormous love that shudders through my entire body is: "This is what my mother must have felt for me the first time she saw me. This is what she must have felt for me my whole life. What she feels for me now."

How could I have ever been disrespectful to her? Talked back to her? Mistreated her or taken her for granted? How could I have ever done anything to hurt her when she has felt this kind of love for me my whole life? Is this what a mother always feels? I am a mother now, but do you stay a mother after your baby dies?

We are a strange group of lost mothers. The ones who had babies but do not get called on Mother's Day. I can recognize the new ones anywhere. Our bodies are pudgy from giving birth; we have scars and stretch marks. Our eyes are wide and glazed. Our breasts are engorged with milk. At night we hear our babies crying. But there is no baby to soothe. There are thousands of us, you know. We wear our dead children in pictures in lockets around our necks. We have blogs where we post their stories. Where we say: Our children grew inside of us. They lived. Please look at them, ask us about them. We want to be heard. To be recognized. We do not want to be brushed under the carpet. We want to be honored, and cared for. We are the face of the worst kind of taboo, simultaneously calling for recognition but not wanting to be wholly defined by what has happened to us. We are the taboo and we are so much more. So are our children. We sense that there is something we can offer. Something about death and life and grieving and motherhood as we struggle to get it out just right. Have patience with us.

Every year, around 30,000 babies die inside of us, babies who will never know life outside, but whom we felt kicking and wiggling, for whom we bought clothes and bottles and diapers, babies whom we will give birth to and hold and name. And bury. More than half of our baby's deaths will never have an official medical cause. Every year we give birth to nearly 20,000 babies who die within their first month of life. For so many reasons. These numbers do not include miscarriages. Or ectopic pregnancies. And they only include numbers for the U.S.—a "developed" country with modern health care. There are thousands and thousands of us. Quarantine the past ten years of us and we could fill a continent. There are so many of us. There have always been so many of us.

I know I cannot get my daughter back. But there is something I like to think that I can get back. One thing I can control: the body. My body. Indira is no longer with me, but I just cannot shake the extra twenty pounds I gained during my pregnancy. Luckily for me, there is a gym on my street corner. I had never set foot in a gym before, but this place had always appealed to me. It looks more like a fitness center that somebody set up in a large trailer home.

Inside those gym walls, I find my new brethren. I let go of my sushi and goat cheese rejecting days of prenatal yoga and with a scarred and overweight body, empty womb and watery eyes, I stuff my earplugs and IPod into my pockets and head straight for the creaky elliptical machine from the 1980s, careful not to look up on the off chance I might recognize somebody.

It comes as a surprise, even to me, the day at the gym when I have what feels like a small moment of happiness, the first shimmer of light, a crack in the concentrated mud that had come uninvited and clogged all the pipes and pores of my being. I am just cruising along, maybe 20 or 30 minutes in, when Bruce Springsteen's "Born to Run" starts to play on my IPod. I turn it up right away, as loud as it can go, knowing everybody around me can hear it, my ear plugs are a piece of crap, but I don't care at all.

In the day we sweat it out in the streets of a runaway American dream.
At night we ride through mansions of glory in suicide machines...

I'm probably humming along and I don't even realize it. For a second, I am horrified that I have turned into my Dad, who loves to sing loud and off-key while clapping to songs on the radio, and then I say screw it: I start to rock my head back and forth.

...baby we were born to run!!!

I love Bruce Springsteen. Just when he screams "I wanna die with you..." an elderly man with hairless white boney legs and a thin beard steps onto the machine to my left and an obese man with navy blue socks and a bright yellow shirt gets on the one to my right. I am sure they can both hear Bruce howling. I start to pedal faster. I imagine all of us are cruising the streets of Grief Vegas, me and Bruce and Wendy and the two guys next to me, the skinny one and the fat one, we are the stars of this parade and damn it if we ain't gonna ride it as far and as fast as we can.

The two men on either side of me start pedaling faster too, like they are gaining speed off the wind of my machine. "It's just us," I want to say to them, breathless and sweating. "Just us and the wind and the open road."

I want to sing as loud as I can, I can almost feel the breeze on my face, can almost feel the vibration of the engine under my feet. Can see America passing before my eyes. Bruce's Jersey, industrial and smoky, abandoned mill towns, big shopping strips, Wal-Marts and Starbucks under big clear skies. I see reservations, and Rocky Mountains, deserts and army bases, suburbs like weeds on the sides of highways, I see gangs and ghettos, urban refugees and rural recluses, beaches with children chasing waves, my mother in the garden and my father at the barbecue. I pedal through the past and the future, there is no stopping me now, no stopping this girl, not on this road between life and death, between land and moon, between hours of grief and triumph, between the start and the end of that breathtaking song.

My gym fantasies are not limited to Bruce Springsteen. I play R.E.M's "It's the End of the World As We Know It" over and over again and each time, right at the opening cords an imaginary portal is opened where I am dancing and singing out loud. We dance in unison across the machines. People on the treadmills do back flips to the beat and land perfectly upright. Old ladies on the bicycles twist their hips and shake their heads. The men lifting weights sing in perfect triple harmony: "And I feel fine." Suddenly Michael Stipe's face appears on the four televisions that hang in front of the machines. He looks on approvingly. People are giving each other high fives, and I am moon walking and pop rocking down the aisles. On most days all of our babies are with us, but they are all different ages. Indira is there, boogieing away, and I am watching her proudly.

Sometimes, other people who have died are dancing with us too. My grandmother, and grandfathers. Jake's sister Jenny, his grandparents. Sometimes I catch Martin Luther King, out of the corner of my eye dancing with John F. Kennedy at the stair master. Other times Emily Dickinson (She grew up just down the road!) and Mark Twain are pop rocking with me. I never knew Gandhi had such good moves! Sometimes I wonder if there aren't a few biblical dudes getting down, but Karl Marx and Bob Marley are the closest I ever come to conjuring one. Nobody stops to tell me they are looking after Indira and nobody pretends she's some star in the sky; an angel in heaven.

But on my best days, there isn't any dancing at all. There are no fantasies. No wild dance parties in the gym with dead children and historical figures. I am just present.

Just me and my lonely, fleshy, scarred body, sweating unwanted fat away, unable to tear my eyes off the Law and Order SVU season six episode playing on the TV, just above my head.

Joy, Interrupted

Navel gazing
by Aliki Economides

I wish to tell you a story. It is about being a mother and about having a mother, and about how these two states of being are connected by an umbilical cord rendered weathered and taut through the braided bonds of abundant love and poignant loss. It is about my mother, who suffered the terrible fate of having to bury her child. It is about my child whose near loss almost buried me. And it is about me, daughter-sister-mother who writes to remember and to connect with life, by honoring its surprising gifts.

This/my/*our* story of motherhood and loss is woven together with colorful, resilient strands that bind me back to my mother and forward to my child. My self-hood is suspended along this life-sustaining rope, defined by these two primordial relationships. Our vital cord loops in and out of us, connecting us across time and space: its site of attachment boring into the very center of our bodies. The three of us bear the sign of our conjoined lineage. The navel, a small, lumpy, imperfect circle and the permanent trace of our causal chain, persists as the memory of both our deep connection to, and violent severing from, our mother. It is a mark that testifies simultaneously to our passive role in our own generative process and – unique to women – to our active participation in the privilege and burden of harboring new life.

Plucked out of life in an inexplicable blink, my sister died suddenly at the age of 18, flipping my family's world upside-down. It felt as if I had suddenly found myself sprawled on the icy sidewalk, the wind knocked out of me, my disorientation severe and my glasses crunched under the hurried, indifferent boots of the anonymous passersby: as if every attempt of mine to shout in protest against this unwelcome truth – every effort to externalize my slow motion rage – was elongated and warped into a guttural cry, met by looks of incomprehension, or worse, indifference, on the faces of those around me whose lives continued smugly to qualify as "normal."

Insistent questions bombarded me. *How can she be gone?* And how can the rest of the world be unchanged by her passing? The incomprehensibility of that jarring, nonsensical disjunction baffled me. How can it be that my dancer-poet-activist sister no longer has a body or a voice? How is it possible that her vibrant, intelligent, passionate, full-of-blossoming-potential self no longer exists? *How can this possibly be true?* The utterly inconceivable had shockingly become a non-negotiable fact. I huddled, sobbing, in the sub-zero winter, gathering the shards of myself inwards. In these matters, "fair" does not seem to be part of the equation.

Twelve years, one month and 19 days after we lost her, I gave birth to my son. I was ready by that point to become a mother and yet I was not. Each major milestone of my life, to which she has not been present to share in, feels bittersweet, no matter how joyously I anticipate it. Eager to meet my baby (which I had assumed would of course be a girl and thus left confirmation of the gender to the moment of birth – the last, big positive surprise we can still have in our era of technologized reproduction), my patience was tried as I passed my due date. Evidently, my baby was not eager to emerge into the wintery world: in no hurry to sever our connective cord. But a disturbing ultrasound revealed the need to hasten our separation. The baby's first challenge would be to survive the birth. (He did.) Then, he would have to be stabilized in preparation for surgery. (He was.) Then, there may be complications resulting in more surgeries. (There were.)

My entry into motherhood was thus grief-stricken and anguished: the traumas of the first two years of my child's life having pushed my (belly) button(s) to the maximum. And yet, induced into being born the day before my mother's birthday, he is the best gift and source of healing I could have ever given her. The deep crater of the loss of her daughter will always define my mother's emotional landscape, spreading out from her center and sending its rippling effects to all quarters of her being, but at least now, this depression is carpeted with blossoms and populated by butterflies. Life does go on. ***Not because we forget, but because we remember.***

Loss is not a singular, monolithic thing. Each grief is different, no matter how well psychologists and grief counselors have managed to describe common experiences and to chart predictable phases. This mapping of difficult emotions appeals to the rational faculty, desperate in its search for understanding. The acts of naming, defining and predicting are ways of containing loss and controlling the emotionally hemorrhaging self in the face of its enormity. All of this is necessary to surviving the pain, I suppose. But still, the heart knows otherwise: it knows that the map is not equivalent to the journey and that the journey into and through loss cannot be circumvented. There are no shortcuts or doors through which to escape. We can delay facing it but ultimately, there is no opting out of the journey.

In the face of devastating circumstances that sever and scar the tissue of our known experience and forever alter our lives against our will, what choices do we have? Compassion for self in the face of the enormity of our loss might be a good place to start. And then? Honoring through remembrance to render the absent present, which, however partially and imperfectly, can contribute to shoring up the ever-eroding contours of the gaping void. Yes, but what then? Look for what there is to be grateful for, as outrageous as that may sound. We will always find what we seek and, thus, to be vigilant about looking for the positive works against dishonoring the magnitude of what has been lost, precisely in its refusal to compound the experience of loss with emotional self-poisoning. At least we have that choice, as difficult as it is to make.

And, so, I express gratitude for the life my mother gave me, and for the relationship with her other daughter, my sister, that I continue to have and which continues to sustain me. Her death, which hurled me, my mother, and everyone else deeply affected by her passing, into our darkest personal depths, has ultimately made us more empathetic, wiser and stronger people for having survived her loss.

Years later, in the aftermath of my child's challenging start to life, and feeling immensely grateful for the robust, bright and loving boy he has had the good fortune to become, I am filled with the resolve to communicate to him (in ways both verbal and non), that he is strong, healthy and resilient. This, necessarily, obliges me to put into practice my challenging ambition to avoid living my life as a grieving-mother-in-waiting; to not be a mother-sister-daughter who identifies herself as the sum total of her wounds and worries. The cord that connects me to my child and both of us back to my mother is now interwoven with my pledge *to dare to trust life*. I understand now, in a visceral way, which emanates from the place of knowing at the center of myself, that to live hoping to be insulated from loss is to live equally in fear of happiness, for every joy carries the potential for grief. And thus, daring to trust life is a resolve that comes with daily challenges as well as immeasurable gifts.

Joy, Interrupted

first morning rays
by Deborah Finkelstein

first morning rays—
forgiving myself
for what I didn't do

I decide
to forgive myself—
fresh snow

her sickness—
why does it take this
to make us close

untimely death—
wish I could have prevented
her fear

white tulips in bloom—
realizing there was nothing
I could have done

last minutes of her life—
the sound of her voice
crying for help

Diving Deep and Surfacing
by Joanne L. DeTore

"How's your summer going?" a colleague asked. The summer wasn't going well for me, but I knew it was a rhetorical question. "Good-good," I responded. "And you?" We chit-chatted for a while and then went our separate ways.

Professionally, life was pretty darn good. I had several poems accepted for publication in peer-reviewed journals, a paper presentation accepted for a conference, a poetry reading arranged at a national venue, and two book chapter proposals accepted. A book, in which I had a chapter, was finally published after about two years of waiting.

Then there was my personal life. I had had my first miscarriage. Intellectually, I knew these things happened, especially for mothers in their late thirties. Yet, I couldn't help punishing myself just a little, reliving every last minute of the month, trying to figure out what I'd done to cause the miscarriage. Had I exercised too much, too little? Maybe it was that glass of wine? Ridiculous, futile thoughts--but I couldn't stop thinking them.

I'd heard stories from other women about their miscarriages. I just never believed it would happen to me. When it did happen, my life shifted in an instant.

At age 37, I planned my last breeding effort to coincide with the academic year, like most academics. I bought ovulation kits, kept careful track of my basal temperature, a temperature I hadn't known existed before. After a missed period, I got the best news. We were expecting, and I was due March 1st.

But several weeks later and heavy spotting, I would be in the hospital having a miscarriage. The male ER doctor tried to console me, "This isn't your fault," he said. "You did not cause this. You will have another."

I heard this over and over again, but I'm Catholic. It's hard for us Catholics not to take it personally. We need a little guilt and suffering, in place of those Medieval hair shirts. It was surely my fault. At the very least, I had missed my window of opportunity. My biological clock had struck 12. Dance over!

After my miscarriage, I sank into a funk. This wasn't like me. I was a doer but, like other literary types, I was a reader. We literary types don't read uplifting beach books during our depression, we read depressing books that have personal - albeit twisted - bits of self-triumph in the end, if at all. Naturally, I reread Margaret Atwood's book, *Surfacing*. The unnamed narrator goes native during her depression in a kind of post-modern *Lost* meets *Survivor*. For the first time, I understood the metaphor of submersion and how apt it was, though I had my mother close by.

For the first time, I talked with my mother about her own miscarriage. She said she was a bit relieved when the doctor told her that she'd miscarried because she really hadn't wanted any more children after my sister and me. Afterwards, she felt guilty and blamed herself. On my class trip as a chaperone, she spotted all that day but just assumed it was her period. Still, she wondered if there wasn't something she could have done to prevent the miscarriage. There wasn't.

I found out that summer that my grandmother had had a stillborn child, which seemed the most painful experience. At eight months into her last trimester, my grandmother learned her baby was dead. I couldn't imagine how devastating that would have been – knowing there was no cooing infant to cuddle at the end of labor. My grandmother told me that she didn't like to think about it and that, soon after, she had gotten pregnant with her second child, a son. We held hands, cried and then hugged.

I surfaced partially from my funk. I started exercising, spruced up, got down to a size 6 and bought more ovulation kits. In one month, I was pregnant again. This time, I didn't want to get too attached or too excited. After some spotting, I went in for my first obstetrics' appointment. My HCG hormone levels were much higher this time and things looked okay.

I went back to work. My daughter, Emily, then five, started kindergarten. I didn't expect this to be a problem, but Emily was struggling. Although she had a very high IQ, an undiagnosed learning disability made it difficult for her to function well with other 30 children. I ended up spending hours visiting alternative schools. After long working days and nights, spending lots of time on my feet, and worrying about my daughter's kindergarten experience, I started spotting almost every day. I called my midwife and she told me to rest, to call in sick at work. I did.

The bleeding subsided, and I returned to work the next day. The following week, I had more spotting. It continued for four days. I went to work, frightened and worried. It didn't help that I was teaching Frankenstein that semester, especially not when we viewed the horrific bloody birth scene from Branagh's film adaptation. I was untenured and the primary source of income for my family, so I couldn't afford to take days off. My mother urged me to call my midwife again and during my office hours, I placed the call. They wanted to see me right away and would give me an ultrasound to see if the fetus was still viable.

I had to tell my boss that I was pregnant. She was very understanding. In fact, she had sent me a beautiful bouquet of flowers when she learned that I had miscarried. She told me to leave work early and find substitutes for my classes. "This is more important," she told me.

At the doctor's office, I anxiously waited for my turn. Women with huge bellies like a fertility goddess idol squeezed themselves into the waiting room chairs. New mothers with tiny six-week-old babies played raspberries and peek-a-boo while I waited to hear if my baby would ever be.

"Joanne?" My mother and I followed the ultrasound technician down a narrow hallway. I braced myself as the technician probed inside. On the screen, a tiny peanut appeared, floating in a dark hollow space.

"There it is," she said. "Is it… all right?" I asked, afraid of the answer.

She zoomed in on what she said was the heart, a flash of blinking white light.

"There's the heart. It's beating."

She turned on a speaker and I heard the tiny swoosh of the heartbeat.

"It's a good, strong heartbeat," she said.

She took some pictures of my little peanut, labeling the parts for me, which were indistinguishable to my untrained eye.

After I got dressed, the doctor explained that the bleeding was caused by a low-lying placenta called placenta previa. She told me that this condition might correct itself in several months, but that I needed to take it easy. Easy for her to say, I thought. I was the primary breadwinner and the primary care provider for my daughter. Laundry, house cleaning, student papers, research, a small dog, and an active kindergartener, and a husband who was not home to help, all drained my resources. Just take it easy, she repeated, anything could cause bleeding – a bumpy ride in the car or even a bout of coughing.

I had another ultrasound at ten weeks and my peanut had transformed into a tiny palm- sized baby, complete with arms, fingers, legs and toes and eventually into a full-term 8 lbs, 4 oz baby boy who I named Luke, falling in love with him well before we met.

During those summer months and into the first months of my pregnancy, I dove deep into depression over a miscarriage and again over the possibility of losing another. I didn't realize the depths to which I would fall or the amount of effort it would take to struggle back to the surface were it not for the buoyancy of a new pregnancy. No one can really explain the feeling of loss to one who hasn't lost, no matter how articulate the storyteller.

After talking with women who share my experience, finding blame within ourselves seems to be a commonality too, even when we know better. Perhaps it is our only way of maintaining control. With this type of loss, we lose control over our imagined future and must revise images of it and ourselves, if we hope to surface.

Joy, Interrupted

RG
by Elynne Chaplik-Aleskow

I am a woman who focuses on what I have rather than what I do not have. Yet, there are moments, utterly private 'what if' moments, that I have shared only with my husband.

We married late in life. Our blessing of meeting one another was like finding a needle in a haystack. This is my first marriage. I was forty-two years old when I walked down the aisle. The next day I turned forty-three. The miracle of becoming us is what we celebrated. Our gratitude for finding one another made us giddy. Marriage had never been a priority in my life until I met and fell in love with Richard who became not only my husband, but also my best friend.

My marriage and my careers in television, education and writing were my focus along with travel. Our life has been exciting, fulfilling and joyous. We have pursued our individual dreams and those dreams we have built together.

One night Richard and I began a discussion on what it would have been like to have had a child together.

"I would have wanted a son who looks just like you," I responded.

I have three sisters and had always wanted a brother. So, wanting a son was a natural response. I love buying men's clothing for my husband. I enjoy the styles and combinations. The thought of dressing a little boy in overalls and suits and ties makes me smile. And if he was built like my husband, he would in all probability wear childhood husky sizes which means there would be a delicious amount of boy to hug.

"What would we name him?" Richard asked me, smiling.

We sat for a long time, thinking in silence.

"How about Reid Gregory?" I asked.

"After my father Rubin and your father Gregory. We would call him RG."

This pleased Richard. He immediately went into a scenario of what it would sound like calling RG in for dinner. The sound of those precious initials was a tribute to both our fathers.

Our discussions continued every now and then referring to RG, the son we might have had. Our talks were not morose. They were discussions about one part of our life we would not have, but we were realistic, always putting it into a context of what we did have and our gratitude for our blessings which were abundant.

Sometimes we would talk about the world the children of today face and we both would acknowledge it was possible that not bringing a child into such chaos might have in some ways been a good thing. On the other hand, would RG have been someone who would have helped lessen this world's despair? Being a combination of the two of us, I would have hoped so.

As a woman, I would have enjoyed the challenge of raising a sensitive and responsible male. His father would have been an ideal model for him. I would have tried to teach him about self-esteem and would have used all my abilities to raise a man who respected himself and others. I would have enjoyed encouraging RG to learn what it means to be friends with women and to love well.

Recently, Richard and I purchased a statue for my sister and brother-in-law's garden. It is a life size boy in sneakers sitting holding a bottle filled with lit fireflies. The 'boy' sat in our apartment for a couple of days until the anniversary party when we would give our gift.

As I entered our living room where 'the boy' was placed and Richard was reading the paper, I heard myself call out "How are my boys doing?"

That is a question I never had the opportunity to ask in my life. It would have been an experience I would have loved to have had. Instead, my focus has remained on the students I have taught and hopefully have inspired. I taught my Communication course as 'Life 101' and tried to teach my students self-esteem and how to reach for their potential. While some people cherish their roses and tulips, I have my prize-winning garden of students, many of whom have stayed in touch. Each is unique and beautiful. I was their professor, not their parent, but the hundreds of students I have had the privilege of teaching will always belong to me and I to them.

I never had the opportunity to give birth and to teach RG how to live, but I am a woman who has focused on what I can do with what I have. In profound ways, we are all parents to the world in which we live.

Joy, Interrupted

A Series of Poems
by Lori Lamothe

Haircut

You sit high on the chair.
At your feet
six months curling across linoleum.

The face that surfaces out of the silver
interests you exactly as much
as the parade of animals crossing the counter.

Each waits its turn, holds hands with its opposite
the mirror as crowded
as a miniature Noah's Ark.

A final flash of scissors and you rise
change falling over you
loose as a nightgown.

I don't know what I want more,
to dip my mind in the mirror—drag silver
in search of lost images

or reach out for the hem of your jumper
and ride along with you
on this current of constant rebirth.

Ogunquit

The beach has its own tide
of chairs and towels and coolers
radios, sunglasses, umbrellas
cell phones, paperback novels
et cetera.

Waxing every morning
waning by afternoon
accompanied as always
by a fugue of conversations
the rise and fall of sandcastles.

As it so happens the sea
is so cold today
that the yang of humanity
is perfectly balanced
by the yin of blue.

I want to swim out to the place
where water and sky meet.
I think it would be blank the way
a page can be blank
the way the mind must feel

when it reaches the edge
of meditation—the place
where all thought stops.
But the tide pulls both ways
and at the moment my daughter

wants to know where the moon
goes when it isn't round.
I explain how it's always there
right where you'd expect it to be
safe in night's pocket
in an absence of light.

Originally published in CALYX; reprinted in Literary Mama

Interior

Now winter is a blue bowl, red blocks,
light that shines familiar shapes.
                    If it snows
we can watch the fire weaving its colors
or climb a ladder of numbers
until we reach the tips of the universe
where planets sit round the stars and tell stories.

Now life has settled over us and the past
is only a pond that's frozen
in the base of a spoon.
                    If I want to
I can skate across its surface
and come to the other side of regret.

Originally published in Notre Dame Review

Camp Out

The tent stands at attention, washed in a silence between cars, as if it were an everyday occurrence to invent objects shipshape and moonlit at the same time. However, it was only an accident. We just set it up and went to sleep inside the usual dose of routine.

I want to write how fireflies hover over the long grass, flashing brief constellations. But there are no fireflies, no field, only this steady rain of doubt. So we shine flashlights under our chins

157

Joy, Interrupted

and I tell you about the time you saw a woman balanced on our rooftop: petticoat flapping in
stormlight, face framed with sepia wisps of imaginary.

Here is a story I won't tell you: the story of this night, of the ghost tent that was supposed to
be your childhood: all the uncrooked lines of your life staked on clean-cut lawn, every birthday
party battened down with the theorem of Till Death Do Us Part. Instead the postman doesn't
deliver on our side of the street and I'm careful to leave any mail minus my name untouched
in an emptiness the size of a bread box. Instead I listen to night falling incessant on canvas, to
water's fingertips typing variations on memory. I defend nothing, am certain of nothing, say
on my behalf only that our untethered future really did glow like rubies, that we slept all night
in the velvet darkness of unspoken secret dreams.

House

that we lived in, one year and six, Nantucket blue,
our windows embers of sun-fire,
the garden riotous and overgrown.

Then the screen door swung open like night falling.
The house opened its mouth and swallowed death's stone.

So you stood out on green and blew one giant
soap bubble of happiness, watched as it floated,
shining us a house painted

the big sky blue of imaginary,
full of puppies and cousins,
swimming pools and birthday parties.

When it popped we saw what we have:
one floor stacked square on top of another,
doors that don't always shut.

Yellow leaves chant sleep across your nightmares.
Candles sputter living light.

In our teacups we read amber hieroglyphs of tomorrow.
Winter with its veil floats down the aisle.

The Wheel has Turned
by G. Karen Lockett Warinsky

It moved the other day with me,
standing in my kitchen
of all places.

Not an extraordinary spot to feel
that wheel shift the story,
the tumult and turn
of life against life,
but I felt it all the same.

Pivotal moments flashed past.
Decisive moments when
outside forces knocked
but the impact was yet unrealized,
unimagined, unknown.

Back when life was moving fast and I,
doing my part to keep up,
didn't always know that
things had been forever changed
by that turn of the wheel;

it was the last look,
the last fight, the final move,
the final phone call.

And so the odd remark or
the sideways glance
was noticed,
but not noted.

Not noted for what it was;
the turn of the wheel.

Not so now. Now I feel that wheel of karma
grind and hum under my feet and
I know exactly
where the invisible but solid
line has been drawn, marking where
nothing will ever be the same, and
where no one will remain in the place
they used to be comfortably found.

Joy, Interrupted

Longing, Loss and Lifted
by Mazel Flores

For over two decades, I have learned to read between layers of thoughts in articulated words about being childless. Be it written statements, spoken words, and expressed fragments of the mind; they all deliver many stitches of pain, emotional distress, and sometimes connotations of being treated as a lesser person just because of failed expectations and interpretations related to infertility. Oftentimes, in the midst of longing and loss, many hurting comments and diverse conversations devoid of tact were delivered by people whom I expected to be part of my support structure. I guess I expected much more understanding and compassion in this kind of loss. No one needs to be reminded of not being a mother, even by people close to our hearts. We can say that now and then, but hurt occurs all the more from people we value, our own dear friends and family and not from those who barely know us or couldn't care less.

Life has its own twists and thwarts on motherhood. The journey of a woman carries several stages in multiple folds of assurances, unexplainable progressions, and shifts of regression. Along with our partners, the joint longing for a gift of life, programmatic results of healthy conditions, eloquent doctors in collective opinions, and financial resources all present; were not all pledges to a successful conception or fulfilled expectation. I figured, not all can become recipients of God's blessings, even if some are truly faithful followers. Or maybe, I just allowed frustration to sip in or submitted to defeat too early in time. For some years, I questioned God for such personal suffering. There are moments when those questions still re-emerge.

For some years, the number of social gatherings I had planned on attending had decimated. Then, I concentrated my efforts and focused on other things like graduate school, creative practice, design consultancy, and academic work to minimize many versions of longing and loss, and to pursue the process of lifting myself. I was productive with multiple preoccupations. Surely, a trained and busier mind cannot entertain additional iterations of longing and fragments of loss. In between those busy years, close friends felt like I was always in isolation. In many ways, isolation is a comfortable option to drift away from new utterances that can significantly equate to unnecessary pain.

How did I deal with such longing and loss? How did I find strength in such quietude and process of lifting? Having gone through the suffering in transitions, I can only recall that first we must search for our own true light, an alternative source of purpose. We need to create stages that will allow us to cross over such pain and loss. The successful cross-over in life is what we can call "lifted," an elevation from one's pain, an extended meaning of one's self.

In graduate school, I once met a female professor who was always inspiring and happy as she lectured in architectural design. I only knew many months later after taking her course that she was childless. I thought, if she could be so igniting with joy and passion in the learning environment, I could definitely be a light in the lives of others. The longer I circulated in several universities for graduate school, administrative work and teaching, I met more women who share the same quietude defined by their own notions of longing. However, never did I see portraits of any suffering from their diverse experiences of loss. Because of these multiple facets of women I have met and interacted, my level of acceptance has taken a positive stride towards deeper meaning and resiliency.

Another stage in my lifting process is manifested in creative practice. In review of works that I truly enjoyed doing over two decades, majority of the works featured children at play, children enjoying nature, children interacting with adults, children in artistic engagements, children in motion, and children at rest, among many other resonances of their restless spirits. Drawing and rendering such images became therapeutic activities for me. The more I drew them, the more I valued my own gifts of tenacity, artistic skill and eye for detail.

I recall in one reflective narrative, I wrote that during this creative period were sacred moments of conjuring the given time and space. The expressive conjectures of pain and inner suffering have become woven threads of light, of hope and one's departure from the feeling of loss. I believe acceptance is the key that helped me manage my own pain and reverse its direction from a regressive state. Acceptance can be a relief from any new fear of scrutiny, and a freedom from any old weakness.

As transitions of pain begin to shift, some colleagues in the workplace will not always be willing to spare us from remembering such longing or loss. In one discussion about length of term vs. the cost of education, the argument led to critical perceptions that I was unaware of such predicaments because I am not a parent. People can continue to hurt us unconsciously, and they can throw out many careless thoughts. However, whenever such situations are presented, we need to rectify people's perspectives, but not to the point of being defensive. Surely, one need not be a parent to contribute essential points of value in higher education planning. Others are needed to be reminded that carelessness in the use of words is not only associated with unintelligible grammar but denotes inelegant taste.

There will always be countless triggers to our pain and suffering. Many will post explicit words and mannered gestures that will hurt us. At worst, others will strike us with myopic versions of concern to undoubtedly magnify more of our deepest sufferings. Languages and idioms may vary from culture to culture, but social representations in Asia and North America both echo the same collective regard on loss caused by infertility and failed expectations.

We cannot change or escape from such primordial perceptions and interpretations. What matters most is that we should not be affected by all nuances further distorting our longing and loss, we must only focus in threading the paths of being lifted. We just continue in pursuing our individual journeys of enlightened purposes, embrace the joyful quietude of prayer and acceptance, and express the vigor of the human spirit.

Joy, Interrupted

Sundered Seeds
by Joanne L. DeTore

I thought I knew you.
We shared so much,
you and me.
I knew you inside,
then out.

We were a pair,
you and me.
Never going it alone,
we trudged onward,
sometimes wearily
but always together.

Then the time came when
being with you was
too uncomfortable,
we overlapped without
space for our individuality.
I ached to be alone.
You wanted to burst free.
Who was I to hold you back?

I welcomed your freedom,
your transformation,
springing from the chrysalis
of our union.

But I was never fully prepared
for your awakening.
You left me sundered,
seed from fruit.
I would never be the same
physically
or emotionally,
both more and less.

I was transformed
as much as you
when you took flight
from my body,
crying from joy and sadness,
we would never be the same again.
We are two now, when we were one,
mother and child.

A Dream Deferred
by Nancy Arroyo Ruffin

As a Latina woman, family has always been the cornerstone of my life because, for Latinos, family means everything. When I first got married 10 years ago, I figured that I had plenty of time to start working on babies. At 34 and childless, I am starting to hear the loud ticking of my biological clock and, now that I am emotionally, spiritually, and financially ready, motherhood seems to be evading me. What seems to come so easily for some can be virtually impossible for others and we never realize this until we find ourselves playing the role of Sisyphus. Trying desperately to push that rock up the mountain only to have it roll back down no matter how hard we try.

For the past three years my husband and I have tried unsuccessfully to have a baby. I never thought that once I decided to start a family that it would be so difficult. Getting pregnant when you actually want to have a baby can be one of the most difficult and emotionally draining experiences. Even more so when it seems like everyone around you is getting pregnant without even trying. I've seen many friends and family members become parents and I can't help but think, when will my time come? When will I be chosen to receive this blessing? Getting pregnant, however, isn't something that we can control. We can assist the process but we cannot make it happen.

For the first two years, while we were trying, I was an emotional mess. I realized that I had to make a choice: I could either wallow in my unhappiness or take action and do something about it. My husband and I decided to see a fertility specialist because if there was a problem we wanted to deal with it as soon as possible. We had the normal fertility tests done. I was ovulating regularly. I didn't have any obstructions in my fallopian tubes or in any of my other reproductive organs. I was perfectly healthy and so was he. Yet I couldn't help but wonder, "If I was healthy why wasn't I getting pregnant?" Sometimes there isn't any scientific data to answer that question. Sometimes there isn't any explanation at all.

Our doctor told us that because we had been trying for so long our best chance for getting pregnant would be through intrauterine insemination. While this is not how I imagined conceiving, when your back is against the wall, you try everything. At the first insemination I was nervous. My hands were sweaty, my mind was racing, and my heart was palpitating so hard through my chest that I swore the doctor could see it beating.

The process took all of five minutes. I was very hopeful that first time. I just knew with every fiber in my being that God would bless me with a child. I remember thinking about a quote from the author Paulo Coelho, "When you want something, the entire universe conspires in helping you to achieve it." I wanted a child badly. It was my heart's deepest desire and, because I wanted more than anything to be a mother, I just knew that the universe would reward me. It didn't.

Every month I went through the same process and every month concluded with the same result, a negative pregnancy test. An uncontrollable anger began to suck me in like quick sand. The harder I tried to get out and remain positive, the harder it pulled at me, taking hold of my sanity and turning me into someone that I didn't recognize.

I began to doubt myself; I began losing confidence, I became jealous and I resented everyone who had a child. Women who were less responsible than me, women who didn't have as great of a career as me, women who weren't married, yet had 2, 3, 4 children; I compared myself to them. I kept asking myself and God, why them and not me? What good is a woman that cannot give life? I felt like I was unworthy, like there was no purpose to my existence despite all of my other accomplishments. The one thing that I wanted most I had no control over.

I felt alone because, although my husband remained by my side, he had no clue what it felt like each month when I went to the bathroom and saw my motherhood dreams flow out of me, my womb weeping blood tears, serving as a reminder of the broken vessel that I was. No one understood what I was going through and I was tired of hearing "just stay positive, it will happen."

Then, one day at a monthly group gathering of women, I voiced to the group how I was feeling. I told them how, despite all of my efforts to remain positive and focused on my dream of becoming a mother, a part of me felt like it was never going to happen. I remember sitting in that circle of women and crying uncontrollably. They all sat there and let me cry. They held my hand and listened to me. At the end of my sobbing one of the women said to me "You must TRUST that it will happen. You must have FAITH that it will happen. You must BELIEVE that it will happen."

That night I went home and wrote the following in my journal:

Trust. Faith. Believe. Those are the words I got from tonight's meeting. As I continue on this path of motherhood tonight will be the last night that I have any doubt. I will go to sleep tonight knowing that I AM A MOTHER. I will trust. I will have faith. I will believe.

The very next morning I awoke feeling differently. My inner voice was screaming at me to take a pregnancy test. I was a few days late on my period, my breasts felt tender, and I had been unusually tired. I made my way into the bathroom, took the test, and waited. I'd taken pregnancy tests before, but there was something different about taking it this time. I felt different and, before even looking at the test, I knew what the result was.

I reached over to the window sill where the test was and in bold black lettering was the word "Pregnant." Screaming, I ran into my bedroom to tell my husband. Before I could even get the words out, tears fell from my eyes like a cresting river. The levies in my tear ducts had been broken and there was no holding them back. I was overjoyed with happiness. After five insemination cycles our dream of becoming pregnant came true.

I called my doctor to make my first prenatal appointment. During our first visit the doctor performed a trans-vaginal ultrasound and confirmed that I was indeed pregnant. He said that my pregnancy hormone levels were a bit low but he was confident that they would increase. At my second appointment my hormone levels had increased and we were able to see the baby's heartbeat. I was six weeks along.

My husband and I were the happiest that we'd been in a long time. He was taking excellent care of me, doting over me and not wanting to cause me any stress. I was enjoying every minute of it. All the time that I spent thinking about getting pregnant, I didn't realize that getting pregnant was only half the battle. The other half was making sure that I carried full term and gave birth to a healthy baby. I was so consumed with just being pregnant that I lost sight of the bigger picture.

As I was ending my eighth week I started noticing some spotting whenever I went to the bathroom. The spotting continued for a couple of days but then was followed with uncontrollable bleeding and cramping. I knew I was miscarrying. I'd never imagined that there was a possibility that I wouldn't carry to term. I felt numb inside. As my baby poured out of me so did my trust, faith and belief. I felt dead. I dreaded going to the bathroom. I dreaded seeing the blood come like uncontainable waves.

I cursed God and what he was doing to me. What God would place a life in my womb to only take it from me? I felt like someone was playing a cruel joke on me. I became a recluse for the entire two weeks that it took for nature to take its course. Almost two months have passed since I lost my baby and I am now in a better place.

I am slowly getting my faith back. I no longer blame God or myself for the loss. Sometimes bad things happen in order to make way for greater things. I have accepted what happened and I am ready to continue my journey towards motherhood because, although it has not happened yet, I was born to be a mother.

Joy, Interrupted

Explaining Metaphors to a Six-Year-Old
by Sheila Hageman

Down by Cumberland Farms gas station at the corner of West Broad and the entrance to I-95 South, the dark pigeons gather on the high wire. Sun glares in Cole's eyes; he wears no jacket even though it's October. Genny only sees dark blobs, but realizes—*those are the birds!* Like it's their coffee shop, their Starbucks, I say. *Yes,* Genny agrees energetically, later on explaining what that word means when we both shout *ABCO* and *The Plaza* like we do every morning on our way to Montessori. Those plastic signs are symbols that we are almost there.

Full of action or acting crazy! Like at Rebecca's pool party! she says. I love how she speaks in exclamation points. But I'm getting ahead of myself, back at the 95 entrance, Genny adds— *they're lined up like people at that chicken restaurant we go to that's like KFC!*

Oh, KFC, you mean? I ask.

Yeah! KFC! Where people are lined up so tight against each other, all the way—pressed to the door—like birds on a wire!

"I Wasn't a Bit Maternal":
Mary Lavin's Critique of Irish Motherhood
by Jennifer Molidor

When Ireland became a partitioned nation in the 1920s, representations of "woman as nation" were linked with the blood sacrifice of the men and women who fought for Mother Ireland. After partition, as Ireland gained political independence, women's "duty" to the new Irish state, according to the 1937 Constitution of the Irish Republic, *Bunreacht na hÉireann*, was essentially defined as housewife and mother. This notion of duty to the state created an atmosphere in which female selfhood was determined by the domestic world. That this sense of duty was reinforced in the official Irish Constitution only elevated the idea that women should stay in the home for the good of the nation.

The Constitution largely focused on the needs of the family; women's rights as individuals were subsumed by their status as mothers. It was a cultural dream of a frugal, soulful, and hard-working populace. In this vision, the Irish mother put service to national identity above her own desires. Where previously motherhood was the iconographic inspiration for sacrifice in a time of war, in this later period the maternal consumer became the passive vessel for the creation of the male citizen: the *tabula rasa* on which Irish identity was inscribed. Motherhood became a contested ground used to develop a sense of national identity after centuries of British colonization. Bad mothers, who either economically or morally threatened the borders of the ideal Irish society, were shamed and marginalized. Expectations for Irish women were limited to motherhood and housewifery, while the stigma attached to unmarried mothers led to thousands of children being given up for adoption and their mothers confined to asylums or "Magdalene Laundries."

Irish writer Mary Lavin's (1912-1996) short stories reveal how the restriction of women to the frugal housewife and sacrificial mother damaged mother-daughter relationships. Her stories elaborate a cultural space for the logic of the female psyche through ethical difference without female self-sacrifice. Lavin's frequent use of internal narrative voice demonstrates the problems these discourses present to the connections between self and other in the mother-daughter relationship. Her stories call attention to the lack of discourse on female desire, the minimal vocational opportunities available to women, and the social obsession with female frugality and self-denial. By denying the self, the bonds between women are broken.

The desires of Lavin's "desperate housewives" are frequently sublimated into one-upping their female neighbors, resulting in a small world of gossip, social hypocrisy, and loneliness. Her stories are ultimately a search for the lost self, and an attempt to both recover, and forge anew, the *terra incognita* of female identity.

Lavin reveals the ambivalence of the mother-daughter relationship in the figure of the self-sacrificing mother. For what relationship between mother and daughter can be forged with a lack of discourse on female desire, valorization of self-sacrifice, and absence of female solidarity and role models for their daughters? Moreover, with the roots of female identity enmeshed in the domestic, to what extent might women sustain solidarity between self and other in the public sphere? Lavin's stories consider, though cannot fully resolve, these issues. Yet, as a writer, she marked out a territory of female consciousness, which challenged the status quo and probed the inner world of the female self, by attending to the mother-daughter relationship.

We can see this challenge to the status quo in Mary Lavin's story "Sarah" from her first collection *Tales from Bective Bridge* (1942). It is a disturbing tale of the destructive power of social reputation. "Sarah had a bit of a bad name," Lavin writes. On the other hand, Sarah is

167

known in this rural town to be a "great worker," and it is between condemnation and redemption that Lavin skillfully negotiates in this story. Sarah bears several children out of wedlock and is barely tolerated by her community, except through her dutiful fulfillment of domestic obligation, her displays of penitent physical suffering, and her regular attendance at Mass.

Kathleen Kedrigan, who possesses a good "name," leaves town to visit a doctor in Dublin during her pregnancy and hires Sarah to clean her house while she is away. Kathleen is warned by women in the town not to leave Sarah alone with the husband; but, attempting to show these women up, Kathleen does so anyway. Months later, Sarah's body carries the burden of another pregnancy, and a letter arrives showing Oliver Kedrigan to be the father. Kathleen sends the letter to Sarah's brothers, who throw their sister out of the house, leaving her and the unborn child to die in the rain.

When the vitreous Kathleen leaves the farm, Oliver is building a border-fence to protect his sheep. Sarah's sexuality, like the "predatory vixen" lurking near Oliver's forty lambing ewes, poses a threat to the constitution of the community. Somehow, the idealized role of motherhood is culturally split from female (and male) sexuality.

In contrast to the idealized figure of Virgin Mary, Sarah represents the unconstrained body and sexual excess. As a mother outside the bounds of marriage, Sarah transgresses the cultural borders of the feminine ideal; yet she remains within the community because she makes herself an example of self-sacrifice, shame, and suffering. Though her reputation is socially tarnished, she is redeemed, in part, because she is a "great worker."

With the exception of her sexual transgressions, Sarah plays her domestic role well for her brutish brothers, who are "glad to have her back to clean the house and make the beds and bake." She gives them her earnings and is the real provider in the family. Though she sins against God through her sexual behavior, she is partially forgiven by the members of her community because she accepts her social position as a selfless and sacrificial mother-woman. When she punishes herself physically during her pilgrimages, Sarah is suddenly heralded as a role model to women. It is as if by tearing the flesh of her feet, she publicly erases her sexual desire. Her constant attendance at Mass also softens the social condemnation of the people against her, "there being greater understanding in their hearts for sins against God than for sins against his Holy Church" (43).

But this community does not protect her from the violence of her own brothers who feel justified, because they are men, to punish her. Sarah's brothers throw her, pregnant, out into the cold rainy night. One of Sarah's brother pulls her hair and, destroying her sense of dignity, de-robes her, by removing her coat. Even worse, he crosses the threshold of the kitchen, which was Sarah's realm. He shuts her out of his sight and out of any remaining sense of filial duty to the other or responsibility. He closes off the safety and warmth of home and she is abandoned, carrying a man's child, with no protection from family or community.

Such violence against women was common and culturally glorified as "male violence against women deconstructed both Catholic models of gender and the nationalist heroic epic." As Sarah's brothers Pat and Joseph discuss her, Pat divulges that "I thought the talking-to she got from the priest last time would knock sense into her" (46). In this suggestion of "knocking" social rules into Sarah, her brothers are subtly encouraged to be violent towards her, by a church that encourages males to keep women in line. Sarah's story becomes a pathetic portrait of a Madonna and Child. Increasingly, in the story, Lavin's tone pulls the reader's sympathy from the more socially acceptable characters towards the promiscuous Sarah.

Kathleen's hatred of this other woman and the utter lack of charity in Kathleen's heart allow for an awful portraiture of Sarah and her baby as a Madonna and Child, suggesting

168

that it is not the Catholic Church that Lavin criticizes in this story, but those who use it to justify their own social standing. The Virgin Mary, as the supernatural maternal, is a spiritual model of restraint and orderly motherhood, and reinforces traditional family structures in the spiritual containment of the body. According to the Catholic Church, she is not the superior deity but the *mother* of God, and in a religion that glorifies the sufferings of poverty and a culture deep within the throes of impoverishment, she is a figure of consolation. There was perhaps an historical need to economize both food (consumption) and sexuality (reproduction). Motherhood in Mary may have soothed cultural fears of the uncontrolled domestic life and body. Lavin's story, in which the narrative sympathy is with Sarah, the hearty woman who suffers the pious judgments of the community and ends up killed for her transgression by her own brothers, is told from a feminine voice.

While moral constructions of feminine "purity" and "duty" were in part economically based, cultural scholar Margaret O'Callaghan argues these constructions of femininity (such as sweeping raids of Dublin's prostitution circuits) were "also a crusade to demonstrate that the end of British rule would coincide with a moral regeneration and the triumph of superior values." In the late nineteenth and early twentieth centuries, Ireland was still attempting to establish its difference from Britain in public discourse by manufacturing ideals of femininity. In this context, the Magdalene Laundries developed from the contamination of private homes and the attempt to rehabilitate prostitutes in order to sexually purify the public streets of Ireland.. Yet, the "superior values and moral regeneration" supposedly displayed by the Irish attempt to differentiate themselves from Britain quickly became an exercise in brutal hypocrisy in state-sanctioned violence against women.

The sins of the women confined to the Laundries ranged from being pretty, silly, ugly, or poor to having been raped, flirtatious, or the mother of "illegitimate" children unsanctioned by the state's marital decree. From the unimaginable removal of children from their inmate mothers to their exploitation through unpaid work, from sexual humiliation to physical and emotional abuse, the asylums were a silent scar secretly demolishing the verity behind the Constitutional vision of Ireland. The behavior of maternal figures of the church was in direct contrast to the vision of the sympathetic, consoling Virgin. As with the practice of condemning rape victims to Magdalene Laundries, this was an overt violation of the teachings of the Catholic Church, which holds that unwilling victims of sex-crimes remain virgins.

The facts are becoming clearer as the desecration of women's lives is finally understood as a violation of human rights. Unacknowledged until the discovery of mass graves in 1999, the darker side of the policies enforced by the Irish Constitution and sanctioned by social "morality," are responsible for the presence of active Magdalene asylums that existed as recently as 1996. As a blight upon the possibility of solidarity between women, the Laundries are only one part of this story. Ultimately, this state of affairs, and the affairs of the state, impacted the relationship between mothers and daughters because of its stranglehold on the discourse of female subjectivity, and thus severely damaging the conversations between women.

In this way, notions of female solidarity between women remain defined by a limited discourse on female subjectivity. Mary Lavin's "Happiness" provides a model of female solidarity in the story of a mother who discusses the "theme of happiness" with her daughters. Vera, the mother, tries to show her daughters what it means to be happy and emphasizes a way of being in the world that mediates the relationship between self and other. Her philosophy of happiness suggests the importance of having this conversation about both the inner and outer world—the domestic life and the private self; the public sphere and the individual place in society.

169

Although it is difficult for Vera's daughters to understand immediately what their mother means by happiness, it becomes clear by the end of the story that the mother-daughter relationship requires daughters to first develop a sense of self. That this self is developed through the relation to others is no less important, but the emphasis placed upon the self as a condition of happiness is vital in this story. The importance of self and solidarity with other women as *the* path to happiness presents the strongest of Lavin's critiques of cultural valorization of female selflessness.

What then is a mother? This story, in describing the search for a mother's meaning, attempts also to answer what it means to be a mother of happy daughters. The answer seems to lie in the mediation of self and other, and the generosity of spirit that is neither selfless nor selfish. Vera tells her daughters that she "wasn't a bit maternal" yet her entire life, as captured by the daughter that narrates the story, shows Vera trying to be a good mother for her daughters. Although Vera's life has been filled with loss and sustained through love, she refuses to lead the selfless life of sacrifice as a housewife that exists solely for her daughters. Not once does she stop trying urgently to make sure they have fulfilled lives. Balancing caring for herself with caring for others seems valorized as the right way to manage womanhood. She must thrive for herself and for her daughters.

Perhaps because of this, Vera is happiest in her garden. Where chores inside the home are exhausting work, her work in the garden is restful. Understanding Vera's garden this way makes sense of her home as a virtual compost of life—recycling and regenerating over the years—and the connection between the female powers of creation and the invigorating desires she imbibes in her garden. And yet, at the end of the story, the domestic world pulls Vera back into the domestic sphere. As her daughter Bea and her friend Father Hugh watch, Vera collapses in the garden, hand impaled on the tree planted as a bride:

> But halfway down the path I stopped. I had seen something he had not: Mother's hand that appeared to support itself in a forked branch of an old tree peony she had planted as a bride was not in fact gripping it but impaled upon it. And the hand that appeared to be grubbing in the clay was in fact sunk into the soft mold. (415).

Vera is removed from the place she loves and placed back into the chaotic household and lives four more hours when brought inside—perhaps an hour each for her daughters, and for Father Hugh. In the last line of the story, Vera dies, and her head sinks back into the pillow, "so deep into the pillow that it would have been dented had it been a pillow of stone." (416). This pillow of stone reminds us of the ways this mother will be forever ingrained in the hearts of her daughters.

As Irish culture became inculcated with Western influences and the encroachment of technological modernity, the struggles for political autonomy erupted, with women negotiating concepts of motherhood. Women writers begin to recuperate female desire and move away from the discourses of duty; some writers, like Mary Lavin, continued to reformulate the construction of the female self to include representations of sexual desire and other-oriented ways of being in the world, as well as highlighting the importance of women's relationships to each other.

Playing Hide and Seek: Losing and Finding My Mother
by Jennifer Molidor

My mother dies every day. As a child, I tried to hide from her; now I'm trying to find her. To have never had, nor ever lost, one's mother means to live in a perpetual state of love and loss, anger and sorrow, hide and seek. It is only now that she's losing her mind that I'm finding her in stories.

A small, gregarious woman, my mother is as generous as a saint, or a thoughtful bag-lady. Although she has little for herself, no one ever leaves her house with an empty belly or without a bag full of trinkets one neither needs nor really wants. For years, she has worked as a nurse with the criminally insane and the severely crippled: people we don't tend to do much for, people others ignore. When I was young, she created a group of volunteers who visit abandoned people in convalescent hospitals and treated them like family. Perhaps she was trying to ease the wounds of her own mother's institutionalization. Her maternal instincts are there, yet thwarted like the fumbling of the blind.

My mother, as she likes to tell people, is *British,* like the Queen. Her journey through life took her from England to Italy to California, but it all started in Ireland. Nowadays, Ireland is a popular tourist destination. People find solace in the nostalgic kitsch of Irish lace, the thatched cottages, small friendly towns, quaint cobblestone, and warmth of the Irish pub as glasses click *slainte*! But there is another side to the story. In 2002, Peter Mullan's film *The Magdalene Sisters* called attention to women's real-life experiences of abuse by a culture that routinely shamed women for their sexuality in asylums, disguised as workhouses, for "fallen women." My mother's grandmother was sent to one such place when she got pregnant without a husband.

Because of the stigma of being born out of wedlock, such stories were never shared with me until now. When my mother's mother was old enough she left Ireland to be a nanny in Britain, and met and married my grandfather—also training to be a nurse. With their five children, they lived in one room of a shared house, which was not unusual for families in the 1950s. My grandma lived there with a mother-in-law who hated her because she was a Catholic, and no friends because raising children seemed to take up all of her time. Grandma was regularly beaten by my grandfather ("fallen down the stairs" was the phrase used at the hospital) and eventually they were evicted. My "grandfather" spent the rent and children's food money on his dark habits of drink, gambling, and other women. Everything from the house was tossed out onto the street and looted by neighbors, including all the family photos. So much pain has come down the generations of women in my family because of this man's selfishness.

My mother tells me stories of her mother trying desperately to hang onto her and her siblings as they were taken away and separated into different children's homes. My grandma was left on the street, penniless. Not until years later did her children learn that she had spent the first winter sleeping on park benches. She even tried to sleep in her local church when it was a particularly cold night, but the priest saw her and threw her out into the snow. She tried to visit the children every week, but eventually her heart broke and she became so ill, they had to hospitalize her. Because she had nowhere else to go, they kept her in the institution for years. Alone, like the women, the strangers, my mother took me to visit in hospitals as a child.

Another secret she kept in her heart was the daughters that came before me. When my mother got pregnant with twins at the age of seventeen, she was still living in the orphanage. She had fallen in love with a young man and for the first time felt a bit of warmth in her life. That too ended in grief. My mother was told she would not be able to give the girls the life they deserved and didn't she want her daughters to have more than she could provide.

171

Joy, Interrupted

The adoption papers were signed, and the nuns took the baby girls away. The loss of her daughters was a wound she bore in silence. She only told me the story when I was sixteen and the twins found her. I saved up and flew to London to meet these unexpected sisters who looked like me and ached to think of the loss my mother must have carried with her all her life. "I only got to hold them once," she said.

By the time she became my mother, she was an eccentric, outgoing, red-headed ball of fury. I was a dark, bookish, self-conscious child. She saw my shyness as an illness from which I needed to recover. She would approach children my age and force me to interact. Because of the emptiness of her childhood, she wanted me to be involved in *everything*, I played the piano, took ballet, gymnastics, swimming, soccer, tennis, dance lessons, Girl Scouts, 4-H, went to catechism classes. And all I wanted was to be by myself and read books. She wanted a child full of life. At the time I resented her determination to make me into someone else. Now, I just want to hug her for trying to give me everything she never had.

What she did have was a volatile temper I could never understand. Little things set her off, and she always assumed the worse about everyone and every situation. "Oh bloody hell!" she would scream in her angry British accent. There were bad times and there was chaos. I never knew what I was walking into when I came home, but it was usually explosive, and often required me to hide my brother under the kitchen table. Mostly, it was bursts of rage followed by gut-wrenching sobbing. Numbly, I moved through life trying to take care of things so that she wouldn't have to have outbursts. When I cried, her constant refrain throughout my life was *life's not fair!* People had ulterior motives and were not to be trusted. *You can never trust a man!* she cried. I realize now she was hurting in every way and had no idea how to be a mother.

Few people understand that, when your mother isn't maternal, the grieving process, the overwhelming and constant sense of loss, continues throughout your entire life. One day in the not so distant future I will stand at my mother's grave. In some ways, I have been standing by it all my life. Although I've been lucky enough to have had a living mother and a mother who *wanted* to do the right thing, she didn't know how. I spent the first thirty years of my life hurting from the loss of the mother I'd needed, and was angrier than hell about the mother she had been. Now that I see she is the mother I have, I'd do anything to have more pieces of the puzzle, more of *our* story, before she slips away forever.

Last August, she was walking across the street to get a newspaper when a large delivery truck plowed into her and sent her flying 40 feet in the air. She landed face down, smacking the pavement with such a force that she broke most of her teeth, cracked her skull, fractured her ribs, ripped her knees, and damaged numerous other bones and internal organs, including her brain. A year later, she is still in tremendous pain, can no longer work, is missing several teeth, and is in massive debt from doctor's bills. Last winter, she went without heat or electricity. Even though my mom says she saw the driver looking down, as if texting, and the cars next to the truck managed to stop and not hit my mother, and even though she was just a little old lady crossing the street, it has been suggested she shouldn't have been in the street where there was no crosswalk and no one is accountable, and no one will help her with medical expenses.

Since the accident, she gets lost, becomes disoriented, and disappears. Her injuries mean she remembers more about her childhood than she does of the past few minutes, though I'm not sure which hurts her more. The accident has all but destroyed her memory and the independence of an adult life. After all she's been through, I don't want this to be how her story ends.

Now that I'm grown, I've lost her all over again. Our relationship seems to be like trying to put a puzzle together without seeing the whole image, and each day takes one more piece away. She's frightened and knows she will lose more of herself each day. By sharing stories, we try to hold on to pieces of her before her story ends. In the movies, when someone is about to fall off a cliff, and the protagonist tries to save them by grabbing their hand, there is that moment of recognition between characters, that look that says it all: the fall is coming, this is it. For nothing is stronger than gravity. Every day I feel her slipping through my fingers.

And so, in stories and sudden memories, I have found pieces of the puzzle that is my mother, pieces of the story I never understood before. My loss is her loss, and what I grieve for, what we grieve for, is that we never had the kind of relationship a mother wants from her daughter. But our story isn't over yet.

Joy, Interrupted

Mobility
by Gabriella Burman

Recently, I sold my car: the trusty Honda Odyssey minivan I thought was needed because of a plan to have three children, whose limbs would grow gangly, an assortment of backpacks thrown on the floor.

I swore I'd drive the car until nothing but nubs were left.

In 2007, we bought the car used from someone my husband, Adam, knew at work. The owner meticulously recorded, in black ink, the mileage of every service visit. The vehicle handled surprisingly well for its size -- crucial to a Generation X-er like me, who swore she'd never own a minivan -- and more importantly, it fit our special needs family well. On long trips, the cargo space accommodated Michaela's stroller, stander and her adaptive bicycle; and it was physically easier to situate her in the captain's seat, in the second row of a minivan, than it would have been to bend over in a sedan or station wagon sitting lower to the ground. Plus, the electric sliding doors on the van were easy to open with the touch of a button while I balanced Michaela on one of my hips.

Michaela was three and our second daughter, Ayelet, was about six months old when we bought the car. Nevertheless, the car would always be known as the "Michaela-mobile," and I put hundreds of miles on the car per week, chauffeuring Michaela to school and therapy appointments and home again.

The van held so many secrets. Michaela often choked on saliva that had collected in the back of her throat, which she hadn't swallowed due to poor oral motor coordination. More than once I had to twist in the driver's seat while going 70 mph and slap her hard on the leg to make her cry and start breathing again.

The car was where she first heard Rossini's "William Tell Overture." In the car, her eyes lit up as we passed through lighted tunnels on the highway. Hers was the best seat in the house at the automatic car wash. After picking her up from school and looking through the daily notes her teachers sent home, I'd ask her about her day. She answered me in sounds and squeals. Her smile deterred the need for headlights on wintry afternoons. The car was where our normal lived.

When we first bought the Honda, I resisted placing a handicap license plate on its backside. I balked at the right to park close to a store because my daughter couldn't walk. Michaela's challenge would be stepping her way, supported by my arms, to the front door from wherever she was.

When Michaela neared age five and weighed 40 pounds, I backed down. A fellow mother at the center for physical therapy where Michaela spent many, many hours told me to take the long view. "Your back is fine now, but you want it to stay that way," she said.

The advice was sound, and, truthfully, ingested easily. After all, I was devoted to yoga to keep my spine strong and straight so I could remain able-bodied for Michaela. The next day, I applied for the license plate, and its arrival in the mail proved a turning point. The metal rectangle in my hand depicted a seated figurine: a raised blue curve, like a wave in the ocean, next to the letters that marked the car as mine. I realized then I was embracing Michaela as she was, and the plate evolved into another symbol of what a family looks like, as I pulled out of my garage, onto the street and onto Michigan's freeways.

When the car began to experience a few electrical problems, such as when the handy sliding door stopped working, we pushed off the decision to sell it.

Then, in May 2009, at age five-and-a-half, Michaela died suddenly and unexpectedly in her sleep. It was just 12 days after our third daughter, Maayan, was born. The car remained, like everything else, a shell of what it had been.

Our attachment to the car grew in inverse proportion to Michaela's absence. But two years later, the radio stopped working--in my mind, appropriately so. Also, the A/C compressor had a "heart attack," according to the mechanic who wanted $1,500 to replace it, just in time for summer. I prayed for a cool season; the children sweated against the fabric.

Adam and I wrestled with the decision to sell. A well-meaning friend retorted, "You aren't that attached to material things, are you?"

This friend didn't, or chose not to, see the slippery slope ahead. If I could part with a car that held so many memories, what would be next? Her feeding chair? Her eyeglasses? Should I get rid of those too? How else would my children know their sister if not through the props that tell the story of her life?

Finally, when we decided to sell the car, I had to proceed quickly like an unthinking teenager. I dropped the car off in Dearborn, in a used car lot parked with other castoffs, across the street from a fast-food Middle-Eastern restaurant and a gas station that sold ice cream.

The dealer offered me cash on the spot, far less than I would have earned privately, but since the CD player, having been stuffed with quarters by Maayan, was kaput, and the A/C had also expired, I accepted less. Standing on the asphalt in the heat, I longed to tell the dealer, "Sell it to a special needs family, if you can. Please."

I took a last picture of the car with Ayelet and Maayan in the front seats pretending to drive. Adam had arrived to take us home. When we turned to leave, I longed to press my cheek against the rear window and kiss the car goodbye.

Later that same evening, I shattered the side-view mirror of my brand new Honda Odyssey, while passing a parked car on the street where I live. Dangling from its base, in a million tiny shards, the mirror looked like me.

I have grown accustomed to driving the new minivan, with all its bells and whistles. I use it to carpool my two surviving children. I call the car "the cockpit" because the leather interior resembles the inside of a sleek celebrity jet; the dashboard controls gleam with possibilities I may never unearth. Maayan, now 2, sits in Michaela's old car seat, in the same spot where I could look over my shoulder and see my beloved firstborn child.

The back of the car, with its empty third row, follows along heavily, like an elephant aimlessly swaying its hips.

175

Epilogue

I wanted a perfect ending...
Now, I've learned the hard way that some poems
don't rhyme, and some stories don't have a clear
beginning, middle and end. Life is about not knowing,
having to change, taking the moment and
making the best of it,
without knowing what's going to happen next.
Delicious ambiguity.

Gilda Radner

"Pregnant 2" – Grace Benedict – Colored Pencil

Lately my husband, stepson and I have really gotten into mythology. In the course of this exploration, I began to see my own grief journey as a "heroine's journey." This journey, according to Maureen Murdock in *The Heroine's Journey* , begins with the separation from "the feminine." This separation often leads women to value masculine values over those more associated with femininity. My own grief journey began with the separation from the feminine, both voluntary and involuntary (neither of which I was conscious of at the time).

The voluntary separation began much earlier than my loss associated with motherhood, starting with my academic interests. Even though I had always been very creative, I was attracted to the more "right brained" disciplines of philosophy in my undergraduate years and rhetoric and composition in graduate school. I was very achievement oriented--my main goal was to graduate and eventually get a tenured position. At the time, having a family seemed optional to me.

My call to the feminine came when I had an unplanned pregnancy during the first year of my marriage. I was terrified it would be an interruption of my plans; I was terrified that if I had a baby at that point, everything I worked so hard for might not happen. The universe ended up, perhaps not causally, reflecting this rejection of the feminine.

Then there was an involuntary separation from the feminine, beginning with my daughter's death and my struggles with secondary infertility. While I still had some aspect of the feminine present in my life by being a wife and stepmother, the physical, material, reality was a firm rejection of the feminine. This is where the longing for the feminine began.

Many of the contributors have also demonstrated a separation from the feminine. Sometimes it is in the feeling of being unmothered. For others it involves uncertainties about whether or not they are prepared to mother under certain conditions. Then there are the different types of obstacles to mothering or there are redefinitions of mothering. The separation from the feminine can also manifest itself through the body, such as in struggles with infertility, miscarriages, and problematic births.

After this separation from the feminine, I plunged into darkness. This descent into "the underworld" often occurs after loss, particularly a death. This stay isn't only triggered by death. Although we never really stop being a mother, our roles may change, feeling like a major loss. The heroine's journey often concludes with a move towards acceptance through the metaphor of rebirth. I am just beginning to learn that acceptance means accepting the challenges posed by life, rather than trying to control situations. This is where I have started to "see the light."

At the end of the journey, the heroine uses her experiences to give a roadmap for others. Many of the pieces and artwork in this book breathed knowledge into me. This resuscitating breath made the "blows" I described in my piece, "Blow by Blow," less frequent and intense.

In my mind, this is when the heroine really begins living. She is no longer unbalanced and is connected to herself, others and the world. In my own grief journey, I am finding myself *trying* to embrace a different type of the feminine than I have longed for before. Also, I am trying to accept other opportunities to mother now, rather than only focusing on the ones I have lost. As an editor I have had the opportunity to mother by, in a sense, birthing this book. I have nurturing relationships with my contributors, being mothered by them, sistered by them, and doing the same in return for many of them.

And, as I continue on my heroine's journey, I hope readers of this anthology will also have enjoyed going on it with the many heroines and heroes contained in this book. Although we never know what is around the corner, I hope this book helps us better appreciate where we have been.

177

Contributors

And remember,
no matter where you go,
there you are.

Confucius

"Mommie Dearest" - Ione Citrin - Mixed Media

Carol Alexander is a writer and editor of juvenile fiction, nonfiction and educational materials. She holds a doctorate in American Literature from Columbia University and has taught at colleges and universities in the metropolitan area. In 2011-2012, her poetry appears in Broken Circles (Cave Moon Press), Chiron Review, The Canary, Danse Macabre, Earthspeak, Mobius, Numinous, OVS, and The Whistling Fire.

Kristin Anderson is a multi-disciplinary conceptual fine artist based in New York City. Anderson's work has been shown in numerous exhibitions nationally and abroad. She has received multiple studio space awards from chashama (NY) and two Artist Residencies at the Herzliya Center for Creative Arts (Israel). Her Internet project was featured in USAToday's "Hot Sites" and Le Matin (France). Anderson was involved in the early growth of NURTUREart Non-Profit, including the launch of the Emerging Curator Program and the original gallery. Anderson holds a BFA from Michigan State University.

Grace Benedict was born in Windsor, Ontario, Canada in 1955. In 1977 she completed her Bachelor of Fine Arts in drawing at the University of Windsor and earned her Masters of Fine Arts in painting and drawing at Tulane University in 1979. Grace has been an exhibiting artist for over 35 years, both nationally and internationally. Benedict is the Foundations Drawing Coordinator at Purdue University and is a member of a Lafayette Indiana cooperative gallery Artists' Own. In 2004, Grace received an Individual Artist Grant from the Indiana Arts Commission towards a series of drawings based on sculpture from historic cemeteries and courthouse monuments, which resulted in several exhibitions.

Nina Bennett is the author of *Forgotten Tears A Grandmother's Journey Through Grief*. Her essay "She Was Significant" is a chapter in *They Were Still Born*, an anthology of articles on stillbirth. Her poetry appears in journals and anthologies including San Pedro River Review, Avatar Review, Pulse, Yale Journal for Humanities in Medicine, Oranges & Sardines, Philadelphia Stories, The Broadkill Review, Spaces Between Us: Poetry, Prose and Art on HIV/AIDS and Mourning Sickness. Nina is a contributing author to the Open to Hope Foundation.

Svetlana Bochman has taught College English and Literature for over ten years. She publishes and lectures on Victorian literature. She also founded Bochman Tutoring to help students with graduate school exams and admissions. Dr. Bochman has raised several thousand dollars for the National Council of Jewish Women Pregnancy Loss Support Program. She lives in New York City with her husband and two daughters.

Gabriella Burman's non-fiction appears in journals including Prime Number Magazine, the Bear River Review, Skive Magazine, and Outside In Literary & Travel Magazine. The essays in this anthology are part of a memoir in progress. Gabriella is also communications director at Big Tent Jobs, LLC. She resides with her family in Huntington Woods, MI.

Elynne Chaplik-Aleskow is a Pushcart Prize nominated author, public speaker, and award-winning educator and broadcaster. She is Founding General Manager of WYCC-TV/PBS and Distinguished Professor Emeritus of Wright College in Chicago. Her adult storyteller program is renowned. Her nonfiction stories and essays have been published in numerous anthologies including: *Thin Threads* Editions (Kiwi Publishing), *Chicken Soup for the Soul* Books (Simon & Schuster Distributor), *This I Believe: On Love* (Wiley Publishing), *Forever Travels* (Mandinam Press), *Press Pause Moments* (2011 Clarion Award) (Kiwi Publishing), *My Dad Is My Hero* (Adams

Media), and various magazines, including the international Jerusalem Post Magazine. Elynne's husband Richard is her muse.

Anindita Chatterjee is an Assistant Professor of English working at Sanskrit College, Kolkata. She received her doctoral degree in English literature from Jadavpur University. Writing is her passion and hobby; it is integral to her life. She believes writing can be therapeutic and that it is the best way to express oneself when no one is listening. Beside academic and research publications she also writes fiction and poetry.

Ione Citrin's art has shown nationally since 1998 when, after years of world travel, a successful television, radio, theatre, and film career in the performing arts, she decided to focus her richly diverse talents on the visual arts. Ione's artistic expression, creativity, and passion for communication have resulted in numerous awards for her painting, sculpture, mixed media, and assemblage. Her work has also been featured in several important publications. Ione maintains an extensive exhibition schedule in juried, non-juried, and invitational arts venues.

Lottie Corley writes about her abusive stepfather in *Trials and Turbulence*, her paranormal experiences in *Truth is Stranger,* and devastating panic attacks in *Within the Mind of Panic.* Her poetry collection, *From Lottie with Love,* focuses on child abuse, infidelity and spirituality. Her artwork is on the cover of two *Prick of the Spindle*'s books. After writing several songs, Lottie is seeking a recording contract. She enjoys golf, psychology, parapsychology, and collecting Beatles memorabilia. She loves animals and spends a lot of time rescuing them. Her husband (a USPS letter carrier), her two dogs and love bird are important to her.

Danelle is a writer and art historian.

Liz Dolan, a five-time Pushcart nominee, has also won a $6,000 established artist fellowship from the Delaware Division of the Arts, 2009. Her second poetry manuscript, *A Secret of Long Life*, which is seeking a publisher, was nominated for the Robert McGovern Prize. Her first poetry collection, *They Abide*, was recently published by March Street Press.

Joanne DeTore is an Associate Professor of Humanities and Communication at Embry-Riddle Aeronautical University in Daytona Beach, FL. Her creative work has been published in many publications, including: The Journal of the Association for Research on Mothering, Art Ciencia: Revista de Arte: Cinecia e Communicacao, and And/Or Literary Journal, Florida English, and in books, *Anti-Italianism: Essays on Prejudice* and *Sweet Lemons: Writing with a Sicilian Twist*. She has appeared on the national *Fox and Friends* show discussing the popular Twilight Series and in documentary film and local television. She makes her home in the Daytona Beach area with her two wonderful and talented children.

Aliki Economides is a daughter, sister, mother and friend and is fortunate to give and receive a lot of love. Aliki lives in Montreal, Canada and aspires to live a healthy, happy life complete with meaningful interpersonal relationships, creative discovery, intellectual fulfillment, and abundant personal growth. Currently, in her spare time, she is pursuing a Ph.D. in the history and theory of architecture.

Merrill Edlund's writing has appeared in or is forthcoming in: *Blue Skies Poetry, Worth Architectural Magazine, Crazy Pineapple Press, Fieldstone Review,* and *Four Ties Lit Review, and Spring vol viii.* Merrill holds an MEd in technology. She teaches high school English and Creative Writing online in Saskatoon, Saskatchewan, Canada.

Terri Elders, LCSW, lives in the country near Colville, WA with two dogs and three cats. Her stories have appeared in dozens of anthologies, including multiple editions of the *Chicken Soup for the Soul, A Cup of Comfort* and the *Patchwork Path* series. She serves as a public member of the Washington State Medical Quality Assurance Commission. In 2006 she received the UCLA Alumni Association Community Service Award for her work with Peace Corps.

Deborah Finkelstein's poetry, plays, short stories, and journalism have been published in anthologies, newspapers and magazines in nine countries. "First Morning Rays" was previously published in the Spring 2010 issue of Moonset, while "Fresh Snow" was previously published in March on the "Asahi Haikuist Network," a column on the website of the International Herald Tribune/Asahi Shimun (Japan). She has an MFA in Creative Writing from Goddard College and teaches creative writing and literature in Boston.

Mathel Flores, born and raised in Manila, Philippines, studied interior design, art history, urban and regional planning, and earned a doctorate in design science. As a creative designer, she experimented with materials and forms by developing furniture design, product and lighting design, and home accessories, which complimented her design practice in interior design, exhibition design and visual merchandising, including the Presidential Palace in West Africa. She joined the academia in 1990 and has held several leadership and teaching positions in the USA, Singapore, Japan, and the Philippines. She currently lives in the USA with her husband and their three shih tzus.

Olivia Stauffer Good is the mother of three daughters: Laurette, Augusta, and Charlotte. Laurette was stillborn on November 2, 2006, and this event profoundly shaped her outlook on motherhood, loss and life. The loss of Laurette and tragic death of her six-year-old nephew, Avery Wood, three years later, inspired her story "The Island." Having earned her B.A. in history and social science from Eastern Mennonite University, in Harrisonburg, VA, and her M.A. in American Studies from Penn State University in Harrisburg, PA, she is a secondary social studies teacher. She lives with her husband and daughters in central Pennsylvania.

Sheila Hageman is a multi-tasking mother of three. She received her MFA in Creative Writing from Hunter College, CUNY. She teaches yoga and writing. Her memoir, *Stripping Down*, was published by Pink Fish Press in January 2012. She has poems published in three September 2011 anthologies: *Uphook Press, Gape Seed: A Poetry Anthology* and *Edgar & Lenore's Publishing House*, and *In the Company of Women: Poetic Musings of Wit and Wisdom*. Sheila has been published in Salon, Conversely, The Fertile Source, ken*again, Prime Mincer, Foliate Oak Literary Journal, Jet Fuel Review, Ginger Piglet Press, Xenith Magazine, and Girls Can't What. Sheila is a regular contributor to Mommy Poppins.

Valean Iolanda is 43 years old and lives in Romania. Her passion is to write stories about life.

Jessica Karbowiak is a graduate of creative writing programs at The University of Texas at Austin and The Pennsylvania State University. She is a native New Yorker who teaches college writing. Her creative work has appeared in literary journals such as: The Chaffey Review, Two

Hawks Quarterly, Blood Orange Review, and Side B magazine. Some of her work has been anthologized, and two of her essays were nominated for 2011 Pushcart prizes.

Sandra Kolankiewicz's poems and stories have appeared in North American Review, Chicago Review, Cimarron Review, Frontiers, Oxford Review, Louisville Review, Mississippi Review, and in the anthology *Sudden Fiction*. Her chapbook, *Turning Inside Out*, won the Black River Competition at Black Lawrence Press. Her novel, *Blue Eyes Don't Cry*, won the Hackney Award for the Novel. Poems have recently appeared, or forthcoming, in Gargoyle, Red Ochre, Rhino, WomenArts Quarterly, The Chaffey Review, The Cortland Review, The Analectic, and Meat for Tea. "The Proud Parents" was written as part of the process of her growing into her son's diagnosis of regressive autism.

Margaret Kramar is earning a PhD in literature at the University of Kansas, where she also teaches. She grows organic fruits, vegetables and free-range chicken eggs at Hidden Hollow Farm. She hopes to publish her creative dissertation, a memoir about the disability and death of her child, tentatively titled *My Son the Actor*.

Ruth Krongold lives in Toronto and is a mother of two, daughter, sister and friend. It is with resolve that she attempts to practice hope in the face of life altering trauma. Humour continues to be an antidote to the negative effects of uncertainty. Working as a psychotherapist and family mediator, she has the privilege of encouraging others to act with consciousness in accordance with their own values.

Lori Lamothe's poems and stories have appeared in Alaska Quarterly Review, Blackbird, Chick Lit Review, Seattle Review, Third Coast, and other magazines. She has published a chapbook, *Camera Obscura* (Finishing Line Press) and has fiction in the anthology *Corpus Pretereo* (Escape Collective Publishing).

Ivan Jim Saguibal Layugan is a Filipino living in Baguio City, Philippines; he is 20 years old, and a freelance writer. His essays have been published by community papers, The Baguio Midland Courier, SunStar Baguio, and Northern Dispatch, and the national daily, The Philippine Daily Inquirer. He was awarded as one of the Mga Makabagong Rizal: Pag-asa ng Bayan (The New Rizal: Hope of the Fatherland) for linguistic intelligence, together with other 34 other youths, where they took oaths to follow into the Philippine national hero's footsteps. He is currently completing his Bachelor of Arts in English language and literature at the University of Baguio.

Rebecca Manning is a "seasoned" single mom (40+ years) with two fantastic daughters, Amanda and Justine. As an amateur writer of short stories and poetry most of her life, this is her first published work.

Ann Mathew is from Kerala, India and she is pursuing a M.Phil in English in Madras Christian College, Chennai. She has been interested in women's and children's issues since graduation, and this is her first step to realizing that.

Janeen McGuire is an artist, a writer, a mother, and a lover of the story of human relationships. She has been a successful Marriage & Family Therapist in the Seattle area for eighteen years. Raising four daughters taught her love is thicker than blood and that creating a mixed-race family leads to occasional militancy. Her husband taught her that it's okay to let go of what can't be fixed, and that it's never too late to have a good divorce; she has a Labrador retriever who taught her the virtues of loyalty, stoicism and endless play. Her work has appeared in Seattle's Child Magazine, The Montreal Review and various local newspapers.

Melissa Miles McCarter is the editor of and contributor to *Joy, Interrupted,* which was published through her small press, Fat Daddy's Farm. She has a PhD in English, with a concentration in Rhetoric and Composition, from the University of Texas at Arlington. Melissa lives in Ironton, a small town in rural Southeast Missouri, with her husband, Dr. William Matthew McCarter, step-son, Britin, and pets, including two English Bulldogs named Daisy and Boss Hog.

Jemila Modesti's art work graces the cover of *Joy, Interrupted.* She grew up around her mother's oil paints and printing inks. Her passion for Art Nouveau, as well as for Gustav Klimt, Alphonse Mucha and Egon Schiele, marked her choice of palette as well as her themes. Her love for English literature, Jane Austen in particular, can be found in the title names and writings in her paintings. Her portraits try to discern the strength of women, at the same time attempting to capture their subtlety and etherealness. Her great passion for Sor Juana Inés de la Cruz is a constant in her paintings. Since end of 2011, she lives in Istanbul, Turkey.

Jennifer Molidor has written and presented on issues in motherhood, internationally and nationally, including a doctoral dissertation from the University of Notre Dame and the Keough-Naughton Institute for Irish Studies (2007), which she was inspired to write because of the suffering inflicted by the Irish state upon generations of women in her family. Jennifer is an English professor at Kansas State University and the staff writer for the national nonprofit Animal Legal Defense Fund.

Mark Moore was born in Southern Ohio. He started sharing his art about eight years ago in the form of murals for friends, family and local businesses. His mother passed away in 2009, and he found an empty spot in his life; to fill that emptiness he started to do paintings on canvas. As time went on, he was painting so much that it was time to take it further. His work fills a gap in his life and hopefully it can fill a gap for someone else as well.

Megan Moore is the mother of three and loves traveling and Tinkerbell. She is 25 years old and lives in Texas. She was inspired by "my angel baby Rain" and wanted "to get the story of my Rain out" in the world. She would also like people to know: "Heaven is for real."

Alan Nolan is a 42 year old science teacher living in the living in North Yorkshire, although he is originally from Ireland. Married with two children, he has been writing since Christmas 2009.

Mary O' Neill is an academic and writer. She is currently Senior Lecturer in Cultural and Critical Contexts at the University of Lincoln, U.K. She has published on loss and art, images of the dead in contemporary art, art and ethics, and ephemerality.

Kim Hensley Owens is the lucky mother of Ethan, 5, and Eleni, 2. Originally from Arizona, she is an assistant professor in the Writing and Rhetoric Department at the University of Rhode Island. Kim has published academic pieces about online childbirth narratives, birth plans, and the documentary "The Business of Being Born", in addition to articles about teaching writing. She is currently at work on a book about the language and power issues surrounding contemporary childbirth.

Monika Pant is a poet, novelist and short story writer living in India. She was teaching English to senior school students until recently and has authored several series of English course books. Her short stories and poems have been published in various anthologies and websites, and she is a regular contributor to *Chicken Soup for the Indian Soul* series. One of her short fiction pieces has recently been long listed for the Commonwealth Short Story Prize. She is awaiting the release of her debut novel and her memoir as a cancer survivor; and she is currently writing a couple of historical novels.

Michèle AimPée Parent is a divorced mother of a 15 year old son and a 6 year old Chinese daughter. She lives in Châteauguay, a province in Quebec, Canada.

Robyn Parnell's stories, essays, novel excerpts, and poems have been published in over eighty anthologies, books, magazines, and literary journals. Her middle grade novel *The Mighty Quinn* will be published in May 2013 (Scarletta Press). Her other books include a collection of her short fiction, *This Here and Now* (Scrivenery Press), and a children's picture book, *My Closet Threw a Party* (Sterling Publishing). Parnell writes and lives in Hillsboro, Oregon, with one husband, two children, two reptiles, four felines, and innumerable dust bunnies.

Valerie Murrenus Pilmaier is an Assistant Professor of English at the University of Wisconsin, Sheboygan. Her research interests include trauma theory, gender issues, Irish literature, and children's literature.

Yolanda Arroyo Pizarro is the author of novel *Caparazones* (2010), edited by Egales in Spain, and *Perseidas*, a book of poems edited in 2011. She won the National Institute of Puerto Rican Literature Prize in 2008 and won the Woman Latino Writer Residency from National Hispanic Culture Center in Albuquerque, New Mexico in 2011. Arroyo Pizarro is also the Director of Puerto Rican writers participating in the Second Puerto Rican Word Festival attended in Old San Juan and New York in 2011.

Emily Polk is a writer and editor who has lived and worked all over the world. Her daughter Indira died of congenital heart defect at three days old. Her piece was adapted from Emily's memoir: "Regarding Little Wren." She lives in Northamptom, MA and is a doctoral candidate at the University of Massachusetts Amherst.

Chris Reid is a long-time Chicago slam poet and member of the Poetry Center's Big Table writer's group. Her previous publications include works in Cram, Rhino, World Order and various online sites. Chris holds graduate and undergraduate degrees from the University of Illinois. Chris is currently working on a stage play about her career in civil service as well as a book of poems, *Word of Mouth*.

Nancy Arroyo Ruffin is a New York City born and bred Latina. As a writer, poet and spoken word performer, Nancy is breaking down barriers one stone at a time. She is currently pursuing an MFA in Creative Writing. Nancy's work has been published in the on-line magazines The Daily Voice, Sofrito for Your Soul and ChamacaArts.com. She has performed at various venues throughout NYC and was a feature at El Museo del Barrio's Speak Up Speak Out poetry event. Nancy is the author of *Welcome to Heartbreak*: A collection of poems, short stories and affirmations about love, life, and heartbreak.

Pooja Sachdeva is a lecturer and a writer who loves creativity in everything and anything she does. She was born and brought up in India, and later completed her Graduation and Masters in English Literature. She also enjoys other arts such as singing and dancing.

Paul Salvette is an author who lives in Bangkok, Thailand, with his wife, Lisa, and daughter, Monica. He grew up in the United States and served in the Navy from 2002 to 2009, with some time in Iraq. His day job involves working at a Thai foundation that focuses on poverty eradication, philanthropy and education. He hopes to stay in Thailand until he is deported or dies of natural causes, whichever comes first.

Samantha writes, edits and translates, alongside raising her two children.

Gail Marlene Schwartz is a writer, performer and teacher. Recent published writings include "A Few Good Men" (Gay Parent), "Acting Crazy: Spying On, Jamming With and Crooning About Anxiety and Depression (Community Arts Network), "And This Is My Other Mother" (Parents Canada), and "Crazy: One Woman's Search for Sanity" (in the anthology Side Effects published by Brindle and Glass). She is a member of the Montreal Playback Theatre Company; she is founding Artistic Director of Third Story Window, a company producing autobiographically-based theater and video; and she recounts and reflects on her stories as a lesbian mother of a son in a blog.

Anna Steen grew up in the Pacific Northwest and never plans to leave. She studied Creative Writing and English Literature at the University of Washington, where she met her husband and best friend. Anna now resides in the rural town of Snoqualmie outside Seattle, WA, where she focuses her time on her family and her writing. Her writing focuses on the role of mothers in their children's lives, family struggles, and the moral dilemmas people face when pushed against a wall. When Anna isn't writing or playing on the floor with her two young children, she owns and operates a coffee roasting business.

Trangđài Glassey-Trầnguyễn is the only scholar who has conducted multi-lingual oral histories and research on the Vietnamese diasporas in the U.S., European countries, Australia, and Vietnam since 1998. She is the very first researcher to have collected extensive bilingual interviews with Vietnamese Americans in Little Saigon, and has published hundreds of works - both critical and creative - in Vietnamese and English. In 2004-05, she was accorded an exceptional-ranking Fulbright full grant to study the Vietnamese in Sweden, and also the recipient of numerous awards and recognitions for her artistry, scholarship, and cultural works. She holds a graduate degree in anthropology from Stanford University and is working on her doctorate studies.

G. Karen Lockett Warinsky was a semi-finalist in the 2011 Montreal International Poetry Contest, and is a former reporter who currently teaches high school English in Massachusetts. Her work can be found on a number of online sites. She grew up in Illinois, and has lived in North Dakota, Washington State, Japan, and Connecticut. She received her Bachelor of Science Degree in Journalism from Northern Illinois University and holds a Masters in

185

English from Fitchburg State University. Karen and her husband continue to enjoy parenting their children, now ages 25, 22 and 17.

Lisa Wendell lives in the San Francisco Bay Area with her husband and two dogs, Koda, a Chocolate Lab, and Bruiser, a Chihuahua. Her daughter is an attorney in Northern California. She has worked for the last 18 years in various administrative support positions at a private university in Northern California where she has established a memorial scholarship in her son's name to provide small financial stipends to students for the purchase of textbooks.

Erin Williams graduated from Hampshire College with a liberal arts degree and a romantic vision of herself as a struggling writer pushing the boundaries of convention. Disillusioned, she found herself a few years later at a corporate job in New York City, her writing merely a sporadic therapy session serving to keep herself intact. She is now a stay-at-home mom, interested in gardening, self-sufficient living, creative expression, and sharing the wonder of life with her two year old daughter. As the center of her life has shifted, so has her writing: She writes now to communicate with others, instead of using words solely as an emotional release.

Jenn Williamson is a poet and scholar who received her doctorate in English from the University of North Carolina at Chapel Hill in Spring 2012. She received a B.A. in English and Studies in Women and Gender at the University of Virginia and a M.F.A. in Creative Writing at the University of Maryland. Her poetry has most recently appeared in Cold Mountain Review and Main Street Rag.

Dedications

In one of the stars, I shall be living.
In one of them, I shall be laughing.
And so it will be as if all the stars were laughing
when you look at the sky at night.

Antoine de Saint-Exupery, *The Little Prince*

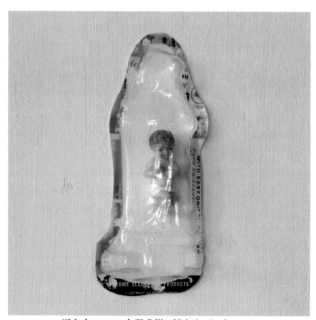

"Madonna and Child" - Kristin Anderson
Package from "Virgin Mary" nightlight, baby Jesus souvenir

This book would not have been possible without the support and love of friends and family. Many of the contributors were also inspired by the memory of loved ones. The following contributors would like to give a special dedication to loved ones who are no longer with us and those who continue to be in our lives.

Carol Alexander
In honor of Kayla, a foster child for whom I briefly cared for.

Chris Reid
Nathaniel Saul Yaseen

Gail Marlene Schwartz
Benjamin

Ann Mathew
Sajini Daniel and Minnu

Rebecca Manning
Clara Kirkpatrick

Terri Elders
Jean Crawford Burgess

Yolanda Arroyo Pizarro
In memoriam of Petronila Cartagena, mi verdadera mama.

Pooja Sachdeva
To my husband Gaurav who helped me in my realization of motherhood.

Emily Polk
For Indira Wren and Bruce Springsteen. They would have liked each other.

Valerie Murrenus Pilmaier
Chavalah Madeline Pilmaier October 4, 2004 – December 17, 2004

Svetlana Bochman
In memory of Sarah Elizabeth Bochman, who died 4/24/04.

Anindita Chatterjee
To my unborn child, and to my husband Pratip and my parents who have been with me through these difficult times.

Merrill Edlund
Thanks to my husband Guy and our children Kalem, Elias and Molly, for your inspiration and your love.

Kim Hensley Owens
For many who shall remain unnamed, but especially for Brenda, Erin, Jasmine, Kate, and Sarah.

Nina Bennett
In loving memory of Madeline Elise Hodgdon.

Liz Dolan
Nelia Dolan Rishko, Edward - Butchie - Dougherty, Margaret Dougherty, Patricia Dougherty, Baby Dougherty and Tommy Colucci

Jenn Williamson
In memoriam of Gail Zion Williamson, beloved mother and friend.

Sheila Hageman
Marcus W. Koechig and Cole Terzi

Lottie Corley
In honor of my husband: Michael Scott Corley Sr. Had it not been for his gentle persuasion, I would have never written another word.

Gabriella Burman
Michaela Noam Kaplan 10/18/2003 - 5/23/2009

Olivia Good
In memory of Laurette Sophia Good and Avery Scott Wood.

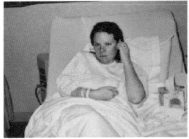 

Olivia Stauffer Good, holding stillborn daughter Laurette Sophia on November 2, 2006.   *Olivia Stauffer Good's nephew, Avery Scott, pictured with his mother, Sarah Wood.*

Robyn Parnell

My father, Chet Parnell (1924-2009), astride his beloved palomino stallion, "Stardust," ca. 1952.

Trangđài Glassey-Trầnguyễn

Thiên-Marie Glassey-Trầnguyễn

Aliki Economides

In loving memory of Georgia Economides (October 21, 1977 – January 1, 1996).

Melissa Miles McCarter
In honor of my daughter, Madeleine Miles McCarter.
(September 1 –October 6, 2003)

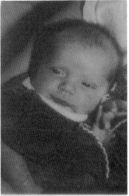

Made in the USA
San Bernardino, CA
04 May 2013